Anonymous

The Child's Bible Question Book

Anonymous

The Child's Bible Question Book

ISBN/EAN: 9783337172961

Printed in Europe, USA, Canada, Australia, Japan

Cover: Foto ©Lupo / pixelio.de

More available books at **www.hansebooks.com**

THE

CHILD'S BIBLE

QUESTION BOOK.

BOSTON:
MASSACHUSETTS SABBATH SCHOOL SOCIETY.
Depository, No. 13 Cornhill.

CONTENTS.

LESSON
1. ABOUT GOD.
2. THE CREATION.
3. CREATION, (continued).
4. THE FIRST MAN AND WOMAN.
5. THE FALL.
6. THE CURSE.
7. THE CURSE EXPOSED ALL TO RUIN.
8. THE SOUL AND SPIRIT.
9. OUR DUTIES TO GOD.
10. DUTIES OF CHILDREN TO EACH OTHER.
11. GOD HAS TAUGHT US OUR DUTIES IN THE BIBLE.
12. GOD HAS TAUGHT US OUR DUTIES IN THE BIBLE, (continued).
13. REVIEW OF THE TWELVE PRECEDING LESSONS
14. REVIEW OF THE TWELVE PRECEDING LESSONS, (continued).
15. CAIN AND ABEL.
16. CAIN AND ABEL, (continued).
17. THE FLOOD.
18. THE FLOOD, (continued).
19. NOAH AFTER THE FLOOD, AND STRONG DRINK.
20. BABEL. PEOPLE SCATTERED

CONTENTS.

21. THE COMMANDMENTS, AND HOW GIVEN.
22. IDOLATRY AND PRAYER.
23. IDOLATRY AND HEATHENISM.
24. ABOUT SWEARING.
25. HOW TO KEEP THE SABBATH.
26. OBEDIENCE TO PARENTS.
27. LYING AND STEALING.
28. LYING, (continued).
29. WHAT IS IT TO BREAK THE COMMANDMENTS?
30. REVIEW.
31. REVIEW, (continued).
32. THE BIRTH OF JESUS CHRIST.
33. THE INFANT JESUS.
34. CHRIST'S SERMON ON THE MOUNT.
35. CHRIST'S SERMON ON THE MOUNT, (continued).
36. THE LORD'S PRAYER; CHRIST HEALS THE CENTURION'S SERVANT.
37. THE WIDOW'S SON RAISED FROM THE DEAD.
38. THE WIND AND SEA OBEY CHRIST.
39. MORE ABOUT JESUS CHRIST.
40. CHRIST TRANSFIGURED.
41. CHRIST'S AGONY IN THE GARDEN OF GETHSEMANE.
42. THE TRIAL OF JESUS CHRIST.
43. INCIDENTS PRIOR TO THE CRUCIFIXION.
44. THE CRUCIFIXION.
45. CHRIST'S BURIAL AND RESURRECTION.
46. THE ASCENSION.
47. WHERE IS JESUS, AND WHAT IS HE DOING FOR US?

CONTENTS.

48. HOW CAN WE GO AND LIVE WITH JESUS?
49. DESCRIBE THE DESTINY OF THE LOST.
50. DESCRIBE HEAVEN.
51. REVIEW THE LAST SEVENTEEN LESSONS.
52. REVIEW, (continued).

TO TEACHERS.

It is hoped that no one will undertake to become the teacher of an infant class, thinking it but a light and easy task, and one that incurs but little responsibility. If such be the views and feelings of an individual that undertakes the training of the infant mind, she will fail of success, and be nearly useless, if not really injurious, to the little flock intrusted to her care. The infant class teacher can be assured of an hour of sweet toil as the Sabbath approaches, if she feels an interest in the exercises of the class, and, what is far more important, the inculcating and development of pure moral principles and intellectual power. To be useful in this department of the Sabbath School, one should *love* the calling, and place a due estimate upon its importance.

It is pleasing to see youth and old age studying the inspired volume, and seeking, by the aid of books and the instructions of teachers, for a knowledge of the truths therein revealed. But it is far more beautiful to see the opening mind grasping after, and fixing upon, principles, that will mould the whole being after the similitude of God. The youth of our Sabbath schools demand teachers capable of debating disputed questions, and of leading the mind along through the dark and misty labyrinths into which they may have been drawn by the many *isms* of the age. But the teacher of the infant class should so understand her work as to direct the minds of her pupils, so that they may, in a meas-are, be protected from the baneful influences that surround them, thus inducing them to lives of purity and holiness. No person of reflection will dispute the assertion, that infancy and childhood is *the* time to make *the impression* on the mind. The sainted Olin once said, the mind of the child should be *preoccupied* with right principles.

It is true that the minds of youth and old age receive impressions, but far more faint and imperfect; therefore the necessity for a teacher of the infant department that is well acquainted with the principles of our holy religion, and can clearly illustrate them.

The teacher of an infant department should not depend mainly upon a text-book or manual to interest the class, as children are much more interested in the words and gestures of their teacher, as they see her eyes fixed on them, and hear the story of their lesson in her own words. It is therefore suggested, that the teacher read over the lesson previous to coming before the class, and be prepared to repeat it to the class in the form of a story or glowing scene passing before them, and then begin with the questions as they occur in the lesson, never leaving the first question till thoroughly committed. Let the pupils in concert repeat both the question and answer after the teacher, till they can readily answer the question when put by the teacher. The teacher should then proceed to the second question, and pursue the same method. When that is learned, also let her propose the first and second questions in succession, and by no means pass to the third until these are both answered consecutively, without hesitation. She may thus proceed with one question at a time, constantly repeating the previous ones until the whole lesson is faithfully committed by the class.

"The questions all learned and understood, the teacher may proceed to the verses appended to each lesson." These form a part of the lesson; and it will be found in experience, that the learning of them will be looked upon rather as a recreation than a task, especially if some such method as the following be adopted: —

"Let the teacher recite one line, and require its repetition in concert until the class can recite it without aid. Pursue the same course with the second line, and then require the repetition of the two lines together; then of three, until the verse is learned.

"The teacher should be in no haste to get through the book. It is best to make the children thorough as far as they go, even if they are a whole month learning one lesson.

"In pursuing this method, the intelligent teacher will of course introduce explanatory remarks, appropriate stories, etc., illustrating the lesson. This will both please and profit the class."

In most instances, the poetry preceding the lesson should be learned before the questions. It will be seen, that occasionally the same questions are repeated in different lessons; but they are such as are calculated to impress the mind with a moral truth, and may not be considered out of place, when we remember the saying of the wise man: "Give line upon line, precept upon precept, here a little and there a little."

One suggestion further respecting the manner in which the lessons are to be committed, namely: great pains should be taken, at the commencement, to make the voices of all harmonize. This will cost some pains and trouble at first, but will soon be overcome; and the sweet harmony of infant voices will charm the ear. To gain this point, great pains should be taken to observe the pauses, and give the various inflections to the voice, which different portions of the lessons demand. As children naturally love order, this will be no hard matter to secure; and in securing this, we gain the attention of the class.

Let no teacher be discouraged if for a time she sees but little interest; for perseverance and ingenuity will succeed after a time, and the teacher will receive a double reward for all her labors

CHILD'S BIBLE QUESTION BOOK.

LESSON I.

ABOUT GOD.

Ques Children, can you tell me who made the clear blue sky, the sun, moon, and stars, that shine so brightly?
Ans.
  "The Almighty God that rules on high;
  He built the Earth and made the sky;
  And fashioned in their various forms,
  Men, beasts, birds, and worms."

Ques. What is God?
Ans. A spirit.
Ques. Can you see spirits?
Ans. We cannot.
Ques. Can God see you?
Ans. He can.
Ques. Where is God?
Ans. Everywhere.

" The Lord, the high and holy one,
　Is present everywhere;
Go to the regions of the sun,
　And thou wilt find him there.

" Go to the secret ocean caves,
　Where man hath never trod,
And there, beneath the flashing waves,
　Will be thy Maker, God."

Ques. What can God do?
Ans. Whatever he will.
Ques. What does God know?
Ans. All things.
Ques. Does he know your thoughts?
Ans. He does.
Ques. Does he know all we do and say?
Ans. He does.

" Asleep, awake, by night, by day,
When at my lessons or my play;
Although the Lord I cannot see,
His eye is always fixed on me."

Ques. How long has God lived?
Ans. Always.
Ques. How long will he live?
Ans. Forever.
Ques. Because God always has lived and always will
-ve, what do we say of him?
Ans. That he is eternal.
Ques. What more can you say of God?
Ans. That he is good, and does good.
Ques. What does God hate?
Ans. Sin.

Ques. What will he do to those that sin?
Ans. He will punish them.
Ques. Why will God punish them?
Ans. Because he cannot look upon sin with the least degree of allowance.
Ques. Does God ever change?
Ans. He does not.
Ques. Because God never changes, what do we say of him?
Ans. We say he is unchangeable.

BRIEF RECAPITULATION.

Ques. What can you say of God?
Ans. He is a spirit — past finding out — always present — can do all things good — is always right and true — never changes — is without beginning or ending of days.

LESSON II.

THE CREATION.

Ques. In the first lesson you told me that God made the sun, moon, and clear blue sky. Did he make any thing besides?

Ans. Yes. He made every living creature.

Ques. Will you mention some other things that God made?

Ans. He made stones, shells, and flowers, and every thing that grows.

Ques. What did he make first?

Ans. The heavens and earth.

Ques. What next?

Ans. Light.

Ques. What did he call the light?

Ans. Day.

Ques. What did he call the darkness?
Ans. Night.
Ques. What did he say of the light?
Ans. That it was good.
Ques. What was made next?
Ans. The clear blue sky and air.
Ques. How do we use the air?
Ans. We breathe it.
Ques. What is air put in motion?
Ans. Wind.
Ques. Is wind useful?
Ans. It is; for it blows ships over the ocean, from one country to another.
Ques. What do we see in the sky in the evening?
Ans. Moon and stars.
Ques. What in the daytime?
Ans. The sun.
Ques. What did God make next?
Ans. The dry land and sea.
Ques. What grows upon the land?
Ans. Trees, flowers, grain, and grass.
Ques. What was made on the fourth day?
Ans. Sun, moon, and stars.
Ques. What are they for?
Ans. To warm and light the earth.
Ques. What was made next?
Ans. Whales and fishes to live in the water, and fowls and birds to live on the land and fly in the air.
Ques. What was made on the sixth day?
Ans. Animals and creeping things.
Ques. Can you name some of them?
Ans. Dogs, sheep, cows, horses, and elephants.
Ques. Name some of the creeping things?
Ans. Snakes and worms.
Ques. What did the Lord say of all these things?
Ans. That they were good.

Ques. What more did God make on the sixth day?
Ans. Man.

"Come, child, look upward to the sky,
  Behold the sun and moon,
The expanse of stars that sparkle high,
  To cheer the midnight gloom.

"Come, child, and now behold the earth
  In varied beauty stand;
The product view of six days' birth,
  How wond'rous and how grand!

'Come, then, behold them all and say,
  How came these things to be?
That stand before which every way
  I turn myself to see.

"'T was God who made the earth and seas,
  To whom the angels bow;
'T was God who made both you and me,
  The God who sees us now."

QUESTION BOOK.

LESSON III.

THE CREATION — CONTINUED.

Ques. You have told me some things about the creation. Can you tell me who created all things?
Ans. God did.
Ques. Did he make all things?
Ans. He did not.
Ques. Name some things he did not make?
Ans. Books, tables, chairs.
Ques. Who did make them?
Ans. Men did.
Ques. What are they made of?
Ans. Books are made of paper, and tables and chairs are made of wood.
Ques. Who made the wood grow?
Ans. God did.
Ques. What is paper made of?
Ans. Cotton and linen rags.

Ques. Who made the cotton and linen grow?
Ans. God.

> "There's not a plant or flower below,
> But makes his glories known."

Ques. Well, children, you see a great many things that man made; did you ever see any thing that has life that man made?
Ans. We did not.
Ques. Can man make a tree or flower grow?
Ans. Man may plant them and take care of them, but he cannot give them life.
Ques. Have trees and plants life?
Ans. They have.
Ques. What kind of life?
Ans. Vegetable life.
Ques. What kind of life have animals?
Ans. Animal life.
Ques. What kind of life have we?
Ans. Animal and spiritual life.
Ques. Will animal life die?
Ans. It will, when the body dies.
Ques. Will vegetable life die?
Ans. It will, when trees and plants die.
Ques. Does spiritual life die?
Ans. It does not; it will live for ever.
Ques. What do we mean by — to make?
Ans. To form one thing from another.
Ques. What is it to create?
Ans. To make out of nothing.
Ques. What can man do?
Ans. He can make one thing from another.
Ques. What can God do?
Ans. He can create that out of which all things are made.
Ques. Men make clothes out of cloth; but could men make cloth if God did not make the cotton or wool of which cloth is made?

Ans. He could not.

No, little children, men could not make houses, ships, tables, books, or any thing, if God had not first created something to make them of. Neither could your mothers get you a single dinner if God had not provided something for food. Your fathers may sow grass and grain, but it would not grow if God did not give it vegetable life.

Ques. What should this teach us?

Ans. That we cannot have any thing unless God help us to it.

Ques. Should we not thank and praise God for his goodness?

Ans. We should.

> "Praise to thee, O Lord, forever;
> Gladly now we all unite;
> Praise to thee, O God! the giver,
> Blessed Lord of light and life!"

LESSON IV.

THE FIRST MAN AND WOMAN.

Ques. In our last lesson you told me that God every thing that you see. Can you tell me who you?

Ans. God.

"The great, the everlasting God,
 He made you and me and every thing."

Ques. What was the name of the first man?
Ans. Adam.
Ques. Of what was he made?
Ans. Of the dust of the ground.
Ques. What is man?
Ans. Soul and spirit, with a body for his live in.

Ques. Was all of man made of the dust of the ground?
Ans. No, his body only.
Ques. How did man become a living soul?
Ans. God breathed into his nostrils the breath of life and he became a living soul.
Ques. What was the name of the first woman?
Ans. Eve.
Ques. Of what was Eve made?
Ans. One of Adam's ribs.
Ques. Where are our ribs?
Ans. In our sides.
Ques. Did it hurt Adam when his rib was taken out?
Ans. It did not.
Ques. Why not?
Ans. Because the Lord God caused a deep sleep to fall upon him.
Ques. What did Adam say when Eve was brought to him?
Ans. This is bone of my bone and flesh of my flesh.
Ques. What did he call her?
Ans. Woman.
Ques. Where did God put the man and woman that he had made?
Ans. In the garden of Eden.
Ques. What was in this garden?
Ans. Beautiful trees, flowers, and nice fruit.
Ques. What ran through the midst of the garden?
Ans. A beautiful stream of water.
Ques. What did Adam and Eve eat?
Ans. Herbs, seeds, and fruit.
Ques. Might they eat of the fruit of all the trees?
Ans. All but the tree of knowledge.
Ques. Were Adam and Eve good or bad when God made them?
Ans. Good.
Ques. Why do you think they were good?
Ans. Because they were made like God.

Ques. If children are good, will they always obey God and their parents?
Ans. They will.

"Lord, I would be a child of thine,
   And thy blest image ever bare;
Deeply impress this heart of mine
   With glories which I wish to share

"But where can I resemble thee,
   And in thy godlike nature share?
Thy humble follower let me be,
   Thy blessed likeness let me bear.

"Pure may I be, averse to sin,
   Just, holy, merciful, and true;
And let thy image formed within,
   Shine out in all I speak and do."

LESSON V.

THE FALL.

Ques. Children, you told me that a beautiful stream of water ran through the garden. Can you tell me what stood in the midst of the garden?

Ans. The tree of life and the tree of knowledge.

Ques. Which of these trees were they forbidden to eat of?

Ans. The tree of knowledge of good and evil.

Ques. How did God say he would punish them if they did eat of the fruit of it?

Ans. That they should surely die.

Ques. Did Adam and Eve obey God?

Ans. They did not.

Ques. What made them disobey God?

Ans. Because the wicked spirit told them an untruth, and they believed him.

Ques. Should children believe what others tell them, and disobey their parents?

Ans. They should not.

Ques. Did Adam and Eve disobey God because their spirits were wicked?

Ans. They did not, for they were made good like God.

Ques. When did their spirits become wicked?

Ans. When they believed the wicked spirit more than God.

Ques. How did the wicked spirit come to them?

Ans. He came to Eve in the form of a serpent.

Ques. What did he say to her?

Ans. Yea, and hath God said ye shall not eat of every tree of the garden?

Ques. What did Eve say?

Ans. We may eat of all but one.

Ques. What, then, did the serpent say?

Ans. Ye shall not surely die.

Ques. What did he say they should become if they would only eat of the forbidden fruit?

Ans. Ye shall be like gods.

Ques. When the serpent told her this, what did she do?

Ans. She reached out her hand, and took the fruit, and ate it.

Ques. Did Eve then know good from evil?

Ans. She did.

Ques. Was she happy after she knew evil?

Ans. She was not.

Ques. What next did she do?

Ans. She gave some of the fruit to her husband.

Ques. Did he eat of it?

Ans. He did.

Then, children, the beautiful flowers faded and drooped; all looked sad and miserable to them; for God did not smile on them now, and they began to sigh and feel unhappy

LESSON VI.

THE CURSE.

Ques. In our last lesson, we heard how Adam and Eve listened to the story of the serpent, and believed him, and disobeyed God. You have learned, too, that God made Adam and Eve good, and did not wish them to know evil; but they, like a great many children who disobey their parents and get hurt, learned the difference between sorrow and gladness. They could now no longer live in the beautiful garden where all was nice fruit and pretty flowers, for God, who sees and knows every thing, came and spoke to them, and said, Adam, where art thou? Can you tell what Adam did when he heard the *voice* of the Lord God?

   Ans. He hid himself.
   Ques. Why did he hide himself?
   Ans. Because he was afraid.

Ques. What did God then ask him?
Ans. Hast thou eaten of the tree whereof I commanded thee that thou shouldst not eat?
Ques. What did the man say?
Ans. The woman gave to me, and I did eat
Ques. What did the Lord say to the woman?
Ans. What is this that thou hast done.
Ques. What did the woman say?
Ans. The serpent beguiled me, and I did eat.
Ques. What did the Lord say to the serpent?
Ans. He cursed him, and told him that he should eat dust.
Ques. What did he say to the woman?
Ans. I will greatly multiply thy sorrow.
Ques. What did he say to Adam?
Ans. Cursed is the ground for thy sake.
Ques. What more did he say to Adam?
Ans. In sorrow shalt thou eat of it.
Ques. What did he say the ground should bring forth?
Ans. Thorns and thistles.
Ques. And what more did he say to him?
Ans. Dust thou art, and to dust shalt thou return.
Ques. What did God then do to Adam and Eve?
Ans. He drove them out of the garden.
Ques. Could they go into the garden again?
Ans. They could not, for God set cherubim with a flaming sword to keep them out.

> "Our father ate forbidden fruit,
> And from his glory fell;
> And we, his children, thus are brought
> To death, and near to hell.
>
> "But there's a voice of sovereign grace
> Sounds from the sacred word;
> Ho! ye despairing sinners, come
> And trust a faithful Lord."

LESSON VII.

THE CURSE EXPOSED ALL TO RUIN.

> "Soon as we draw our infant breath,
> The seeds of sin grow up for death;
> Thy law demands a perfect heart,
> But we're defiled in every part."

Ques. Did Adam and Eve die as God had told them?
Ans. They did, for the image of God died in them.
Ques. Is this what God meant when he said, Thou shalt surely die?
Ans. It is; for,

> "Plunged in a gulf of dark despair,
> We wretched sinners lay,
> Without one cheering beam of hope,
> Or spark of glimmering day."

Ques. Did he not mean more than this?
Ans. He meant that their bodies should become sickly and die too.
Ques. Which is to be lamented most, that our bodies die, or that we have lost God's image on our souls?
Ans. That we have lost God's image on our souls.
Ques. What is it to have his image on our souls?
Ans. To be good like God.
Ques. Can we go to heaven if we have not his image?
Ans. We cannot.
Ques. Could Adam and Eve have gone to heaven if God had left them after they had disobeyed him?
Ans. They could not.
Ques. Do you not think that they were afraid that they would be left to the wicked spirit?
Ans. We do.
Ques. Does God pity wicked people, and try to make them good and happy?
Ans. He does.

"With pitying eyes the Prince of grace
Beheld our helpless grief;
He saw, and (O amazing love!)
He ran to our relief."

Ques. What did he do for Adam and Eve?
Ans. He gave them a promise of mercy.
Ques. What was this promise?
Ans. That his own Son would come into the world
Ques. Why should he come into the world?
Ans. To break the power of the wicked spirit.
Ques. What more was he to do?
Ans. Save the world from sin.
Ques. Are we all sinners?
Ans. We have all sinned, and come short of the glory of God.
Ques. How could Adam and Eve be saved?
Ans. In believing God's promise.
Ques. How are we to be saved?
Ans. In believing on the Son of God.

"Angels, assist our mighty joys;
Strike all your harps of gold;
But when you raise your highest notes,
His love can ne'er be told!"

LESSON VIII.

THE SOUL AND SPIRIT.

"A charge to keep I have,
  A God to glorify;
A never-dying soul to save,
  And fit it for the sky."

Ques. How many senses have you?
Ans. Five.
Ques. What are they?
Ans. Hearing, seeing, smelling, tasting, and feeling.
Ques. Should you have these senses if you had no spirit?
Ans. We should not.
Ques. Did you ever see a dead boy or girl?
Ans. Yes.
Ques. Well, they had eyes, ears, and hands, had they not?
Ans. Yes; but they could not see with their eyes, or hear with their ears, nor move their hands or feet.
Ques. Why not?
Ans. Because their souls had left their bodies.
Ques. What is your soul?
Ans. Something within me, that makes me love and wish and think.

Ques. What will become of your bodies when your souls leave them?
Ans. They will die, and moulder in the ground
Ques. Must all men die?
Ans. Yes.

> "Death enters, and there 's no defence;
> His time there 's none can tell;
> He 'll in a moment call thee hence,
> To heaven, or down to hell."

Ques. How long will your souls live?
Ans. Forever: as long as God shall live.
Ques. What will become of your soul when your body dies?
Ans. It will go to God, who gave it.
Ques. Why will it go to God?
Ans. To be judged.
Ques. Do little children die?
Ans. Yes.

> "Millions of infant souls compose
> The family above."

Ques. Where will your spirits live if you have been good?
Ans. In a happy place.
Ques. If you are wicked and bad, where will they live?
Ans. In a place of dreadful misery.
Ques. Does God know if we have been good or bad?
Ans. He does.

> "How careful, then, ought I to live!
> With what religious fear,
> Who such a strict account must give
> For my behavior here!"

Ques. Why do you think he will know if you have been good or bad?
Ans. He knows all things.
Ques. Shall we know as much as we do now when our spirits have left our bodies?
Ans. We shall.

Ques Shall we feel as happy as we now do, if we have been good?
Ans. O yes!

> If I shall reach that happy place,
> And be forever bless'd,
> Then I shall see my Father's face,
> And in his bosom rest."

Ques And shall we be sad if we have been bad?
Ans Yes.

> "Infinite joy or endless woe
> Attends on every breath,
> And yet how unconcerned we go
> Upon the brink of death!"

LESSON IX.

OUR DUTIES TO GOD.

Ques. Little children, who has done very much for us?
Ans.

> "His name is God: He gave me birth,
> And every living thing on earth;
> And every tree and every plant that grows,
> To the same hand its being owes."

Ques. How should we feel towards God?
Ans. Feel thankful to him, and love him.
Ques. Why should we love him?
Ans. Because he has told us to love him.
Ques. What has he commanded us to give him?
Ans. Our hearts.
Ques. How can we give our hearts to him?
Ans. We can tell him that we will obey him and love him, and ask him to take our wicked hearts.
Ques. Will he take our wicked hearts?
Ans. He will, and give us better ones.
Ques. What does he say of those that love him?
Ans. I love those that love me.
Ques. What of those that seek him early?
Ans. They shall find me.
Ques. What do we owe to God besides love?
Ans. Obedience and fear.
Ques. Why should we fear God?
Ans. Because he is pleased with those that fear him.
Ques. Can you fear and love God too?
Ans. We can; for if we love him we shall fear to displease him.
Ques. If you love God, how will you act with reference to him?
Ans. We shall obey him.
Ques. What is the beginning of wisdom?
Ans. The fear of the Lord.
Ques. If you knew a man that could hurt you, and would hurt you if you did not obey him, how should you regard him?
Ans. With fear.
Ques. Well, if he was very kind, and gave you everything to make you happy, how should you regard him?
Ans. With love.
Ques. Then you would both love and fear him, should you not?
Ans. We should

Ques. Little children, God has given you all your good things, and he can destroy you and make you unhappy forever. Then how should you feel towards him?

Ans. We should love, and fear him too.

Ques. What is the whole duty of man?

Ans. To fear God, and keep his commandments.

Ques. For what did God make man?

Ans. To love and obey him, and be happy forever.

Ques. If we are not finally happy, will it be because God has not loved us?

Ans. It will not.

"When I look up to yonder sky,
So pure, so bright, so wondrous high,
I think of one I cannot see,
But one who sees, and cares for me.

"'T is he my daily food provides,
And all that I require besides;
And when I close my slumbering eyes,
I sleep in peace, for he is nigh.

"Then surely I should ever love
This gracious God who reigns above;
For very kind indeed is he,
To love a little child like me."

LESSON X.

DUTIES OF CHILDREN TO EACH OTHER.

Ques. You have told me some of our duties to God; now can you tell me some of your duties to each other?
Ans.
"Deal with another, as you 'd have
Another deal with you;
What you 're unwilling to receive,
Be sure you never do."

Ques. If a little boy should be unkind to you and hate you, should you try to make him unhappy?
Ans. We should be kind to him, and try to make him love us.

Ques. Should you be offended with naughty children when they try to vex and teaze you?
Ans.
"I 'll not wittingly offend,
Nor be easily offended;
What 's amiss I 'll strive to mend,
And endure what can't be mended.'

Ques. What are we not to do when we are called by hard names?

Ans. We must not call hard names in return.

Ques. If your little playmates call you hard names, what should you do?

Ans.
"If I meet with railing tongues,
  Why should I return them railing?
Since I best revenge my wrongs,
  By my patience never failing."

Ques. What is your duty to the poor?

Ans. Help them if I can.

Ques. How should you feel for them if you cannot help them?

Ans. Pity them.

Ques. If you see little boys and girls that have on poor clothes, should you laugh at them and be proud of yours?

Ans. We should not, for —

"The art of dress did ne'er begin
 Till Eve, our mother, learned to sin."

Ques. There are a great many children that have no home, no father and mother, or any one to care for them; and their clothes get ragged, and they are taught to steal and beg their food. None speaks kindly to them, and they feel that every one dislikes them; and sometimes, when they meet little children that are dressed well they feel ashamed. Do you think that good boys and girls will laugh at them?

Ans. They would not.

Ques. Sometimes naughty children do laugh at these poor children, and that makes them angry, and then they speak wicked words, and try to quarrel with them; but if these poor children were taught better, they would not do so, though they would feel very bad to be laughed at. Now can you do any thing to help these poor children?

Ans. We can give our pennies to the missionary, **and** he will teach them better.

Ques. Can he not do more than this?

Ans. Yes; he can get homes for them, and some one to take care of them.

Ques. Then is it not your duty to give your pennies to the missionary, instead of buying candy with them?

Ans. It is.

> "Children, work and lead the blind,
> By a careful hand and kind,
> Guide them from the ills of earth,
> To the joys of heavenly birth.
>
> "Children, love, and gentle prove;
> Let no tongue in anger move;
> Let no hands in anger strike;
> To your lovely Lord be like.
>
> "Children, think; and on life's past
> Muse, to fit you for its last;
> And when death for you shall come,
> Heaven shall be your happy home"

LESSON XI.

GOD HAS TAUGHT US OUR DUTIES IN THE BIBLE.

Little children, you have learned some of your duties to God and each other.

Ques. What book teaches us these things?
Ans. The Bible.
Ques. Does the Bible teach us the truth?
Ans. It does, for it is God's own words to us.
Ques. What can you say of the Bible?
Ans. It is a precious book indeed.

> "It is a precious book indeed,
> Happy the child that loves to read;
> 'T is God's own word that he has given,
> To show our souls the way to heaven."

Ques. Who wrote the Bible?
Ans. Good men.
Ques. Who told them what to write?
Ans. God.
Ques. How did he make them understand what to write?
Ans. By his Holy Spirit.
Ques. Can you tell me the names of some of the good men that wrote the Bible?
Ans. Moses and Joshua.
Ques. Did they not write except God told them?
Ans. They did not.
Ques. The Bible is divided into two parts; what are they called?
Ans. Old and New Testaments.
Ques. How many books in the Old Testament?
Ans. Thirty-nine.
Ques. What does the Old Testament teach us?
Ans. 1st. That God created all things. 2d. That he made all things good. 3d. That God loves goodness, and hates sin. 4th. That he cares for good people. 5th. That he will punish the wicked. 6th. It teaches our duty to God and man.
Ques. Who wrote the book that contains the commandments?
Ans. Moses.
Ques. Whom do we suppose wrote the history of the kings in Israel?
Ans. Ezra the scribe.
Ques. Who wrote psalms of praise to God?
Ans. David, the pious king.
Ques. Who wrote wise sayings?
Ans. Solomon, the king and wisest man.
Ques. Who wrote of the visions they saw, and told what was to take place in the world?
Ans. Daniel, Jeremiah, and many more.
Ques. What can you say of Daniel?

Ans. He was thrown into a den of wild lions.
Ques. What can you say of Jeremiah?
Ans. He was thrown into a prison.
Ques. Why was Daniel thrown into the den of lions?
Ans. Because he prayed to God.
Ques. Why was Jeremiah thrown into prison?
Ans. Because he spoke as God told him to.
Ques. What were these men called?
Ans. Prophets.
Ques. What is a prophet?
Ans. One that tells what is to take place.
Ques. Should you not like to be good like these men that talked with God and knew his will?
Ans. O yes.

"Daniel's wisdom may we know,
Job's submission may we show,
Moses' meekness, Joshua's zeal,
Peter's fervent spirit feel.

"Most of all, may I pursue
The example Jesus drew;
In my life and conduct show
How he lived and walked below."

LESSON XII.

GOD HAS TAUGHT US OUR DUTIES IN THE BIBLE --- CONTINUED.

Ques. You have told me something about the Old Testament. Can you tell me how many books in the New Testament?

Ans. Twenty-seven.

Ques. Who wrote the four first books?

Ans. Matthew, Mark, Luke, and John.

Ques. What did they write about?

Ans. About Jesus Christ, and what he did and taught.

Ques. Did they know him?

Ans. They did, for they learned of him.

Ques. Does the Old Testament speak of Jesus Christ?

Ans. It does. It tells of his coming into the world to save it from sin.

Ques. What does the prophet Isaiah call him?

Ans. The Prince of peace.

Ques. Did Isaiah write in the Old or New Testament?
Ans. In the Old Testament.
Ques. Did the prophets tell of any one besides Christ that should come?
Ans. They wrote of John the Baptist.
Ques. Who was John the Baptist?
Ans. The man that prepared the way for Jesus Christ.
Ques. What more does the New Testament teach us?
Ans. It tells us of the apostles and the end of the world.
Ques. What else does the New Testament contain?
Ans. Many letters to good people.
Ques. Who wrote a great many of the letters?
Ans. St. Paul.
Ques. Who was St. Paul?
Ans. He was a very wise and good man.
Ques. What was he before he saw Jesus?
Ans. A very wicked man.
Ques. What did he become afterwards?
Ans. A preacher.
Ques. What does the New Testament teach?
Ans. 1st. That Christ came into the world. 2d. Was crucified for the sins of the world. 3d. That because Christ suffered we may be happy forever. 4th. That we must obey his teachings if we would be happy. 5th. If we do not obey him, we shall be lost.
Ques. What does the Bible tell us?
Ans.
"It tells us how the world was made,
And how good men the Lord obeyed;
It points to heaven, where angels dwell,
And warns us to escape from hell."

Ques. Could any but good men have written the Bible?
Ans. They could not.
Ques. What does God say he will do to those that take any thing from the Bible?

Ans. That he will take their names from the book of life.

Ques. And what has he said he would do to those that should write more than he has told them to write?

Ans. That he would add to them the plagues that are written about in the Bible.

> "The Bible! the Bible! more precious than gold
> The hopes and the glories its pages unfold;
> It speaks of salvation — wide opens the door:
> Its offers are free to the rich and the poor.
>
> "The Bible! the Bible! blest volume of truth,
> How sweetly it smiles on the season of youth;
> It bids us seek early the pearl of great price,
> Ere the heart is enslaved in the bondage of vice.
>
> "The Bible! the Bible! the valleys shall ring,
> And hill-tops re-echo the notes that we sing:
> Our banners, inscribed with its precepts and rules,
> Shall long wave in triumph, the joy of our schools."

LESSON XIII.

REVIEW OF THE TWELVE PRECEDING LESSONS.

Ques. What can you say of God?

Ans. He is a spirit — past finding out; can do all things good; is always right and true; never changes; is without beginning or ending of days.

Ques. Name some things that God has made?

Ans. The sun and moon and stars, besides every living creature.

Ques. How long was God in making all things?

Ans. Six days.

Ques. What was made first?

Ans. The heavens and the earth.

Ques. What was made last?

Ans. Man.

Ques. Of what did he make him?
Ans. Of the dust of the earth.
Ques. What do we breathe?
Ans. The air.
Ques. What is air put in motion?
Ans. Wind.
Ques. What if the air should be taken **away**?
Ans. Then we could not breathe.
Ques. What is it to create?
Ans. To make out of nothing.
Ques. What has God done?
Ans. He created that of which every thing is made.
Ques. What can man do?
Ans. He can make one thing of another.
Ques. What was the name of the first man?
Ans. Adam.
Ques. Name of the first woman?
Ans. Eve.
Ques. Where were they placed?
Ans. In the garden of Eden.
Ques. What was given to them for food?
Ans. Herbs, seeds, and fruit.
Ques. What did they do?
Ans. They disobeyed God.
Ques. How were they punished?
Ans. God cursed them, and drove them from the **gar**den.
Ques. Did they die as the Lord had told them?
Ans. They did — their bodies became sickly and died and the image of God died in them.
Ques. How did Adam and Eve feel after they had broken God's commands?
Ans. They were ashamed, and hid **themselves**.
Ques. What were they exposed to?
Ans. Eternal death.
Ques. Does the Lord pity the wicked?
Ans. He does.

Ques. What is his language to sinners?
Ans.

> "Sinners, turn, why will ye die?
> God, your Maker, asks you why?
> God, who did your being give,
> Made you with himself to live."

Ques. What did he do for Adam and Eve?
Ans. He gave them a promise of mercy.
Ques How could they be saved?
Ans. By faith in the promised seed.
Ques. What was they to believe?
Ans. That Christ was to come into the world to save it from sin.
Ques. How can we be saved?
Ans. In believing on Christ.

> "Jesus, while thou wast below,
> Thou to all thy love didst show;
> And didst say to such as we,
> Suffer them to come to me.
>
> "Wilt thou not pronounce us blest?
> Let on us thy blessing rest;
> Grant that we may be of those
> Who thy kingdom shall compose."

LESSON XIV.

REVIEW — CONTINUED.

Ques. What is your soul?
Ans. Something within me that makes me love and wish and breathe.
Ques. How long will your soul live?
Ans. Forever.
Ques. What will become of your body when your soul and spirit leave it?

Ans. It will moulder in the earth.

> "Corruption, earth, and worms
> Shall but refine this flesh,
> Till my triumphant spirit comes
> To put it on afresh."

Ques. What is your body?
Ans. A cage for my soul.
Ques. Will your bodies ever be made **alive?**
Ans. They will at the last day.
Ques. Who will raise our bodies?
Ans. Jesus Christ.
Ques. What kind of bodies shall we have?
Ans. Glorious bodies.

> "Arrayed in glorious grace
> Shall these vile bodies shine;
> And every shape and every face
> Be heavenly and divine."

Ques. Where will your soul go when you die?
Ans. To God.
Ques. What will he do with them?
Ans. If we have been good, he will take them to heaven; if we have been wicked, he will send them to a place of punishment.
Ques. Does God like to punish the wicked?
Ans. O no!

> "He cannot bear to see
> A wretched sinner die."

Ques. From whom do we receive all our good things?
Ans. From God.
Ques. What are our duties to him?
Ans. 1st. Obey him; because he made us, and keeps us. 2d. Love him; because he has done so much for us. 3d. Trust him; because he will never fail us. 4th. Fear him; because he is holy, and will punish sinners. 5th Pray to him; for he alone can give us eternal life.
Ques. What is the whole duty of man?
Ans. Fear God, and keep his commandments.

Ques. Name some duties we owe to each other?
Ans. 1st. Be kind to all. 2d. Offend none. 3d. Pity the poor. 4th. Give our pennies to the missionary for the poor children.

Ques. How should we regard the faults of our companions?

> " Be to their faults a little blind,
> Be to their virtues very kind."

Ques. Where has God taught us our duties?
Ans. In the Bible.
Ques. How is the Bible divided?
Ans. Into the Old and New Testaments.
Ques. Who wrote the Bible?
Ans. Good men.
Ques. Who taught them what to write?
Ans. God did, by his Holy Spirit.
Ques. What did the prophets write?
Ans. Of things to come.
Ques. Of what does the New Testament tell us?
Ans. Of Jesus Christ and heaven.
Ques. Will you read the Bible when learnt how?

> " Holy Bible, book divine;
> Precious treasure! thou art mine;
> Mine to tell me whence I came,
> Mine to teach me what I am.
> Mine to comfort in distress,
> If the Holy Spirit bless;
> Mine to show of living faith
> Man can triumph over death."

LESSON XV.

CAIN AND ABEL.

Little children, you have learned that God created all things, and that all that he made was good. You have learned how Adam and Eve disobeyed God, and brought sin and death into the world, and that while they were in this sad condition, God made them a promise of mercy; and told them how they might be saved. You have heard how the Bible was given to us to teach us our duties to God and man; and now I wish you would tell me something about Adam's children.

Ques. Were Adam's children wicked?
Ans. They were.

> 'Lord, we are vile, conceived in sin,
> And born unholy and unclean:
> Sprung from the man whose guilty fall
> Corrupts his race and taints us all.''

Ques. Can you name some of his children?
Ans. Cain and Abel.
Ques. Can you tell me any thing about Cain?

Ans. He ploughed and planted the ground.
Ques. What did Abel do?
Ans. He took care of sheep and lambs.
Ques. What did they do on Sunday?
Ans. They worshipped God.
Ques. How did they worship him?
Ans. They brought, of the fruit of the ground, an offering to the Lord.
Ques. What was this offering made of?
Ans. Fine flour and sweet oil.
Ques. Why did they bring this?
Ans. To show that they thanked him for his care.
Ques. Should they have done more than this?
Ans. They should have confessed their sins.

"O may my broken, contrite heart.
Timely my sins lament,
And early, with repentant tears,
Eternal woe prevent."

Ques. What should they have done after confessing their sins?
Ans. They should have asked God to have forgiven them.
Ques. Should we confess to God that we are sinners and ask his forgiveness?
Ans. We must if we wish to be saved.
Ques. Did Cain and Abel do so?
Ans. Abel did, but Cain did not.
Ques. Was God pleased with Abel?
Ans. He was, and he smiled on him.
Ques. How did he look on Cain?
Ans. He frowned on him.
Ques. What did Abel bring to God to show that he was sinful, and wished to be forgiven?
Ans. A lamb, the firstling of the flock.

"Behold, for me the victim bleeds.
His wounds are open wide;
For me the blood of sprinkling pleasd,
And speaks me justified."

Ques. What is the firstling of the flock?
Ans. The oldest lamb.
Ques. Would God have loved Cain if he had brought a lamb as Abel did?
Ans. He would.
Ques. How did Cain feel when he saw that God loved Abel more than he did him?
Ans. He was angry with Abel.
Ques. What did he do to Abel?
Ans. He rose up one day, when he was in the field, and killed him.
Ques. If Cain had gone to the Lord, and told him that his spirit was wicked, and asked him for a good spirit, do you think he would have killed his brother?
Ans. We do not.

LESSON XVI.

CAIN AND ABEL — CONTINUED.

In the last lesson, we learned that Cain did not worship God as he ought, and that the Lord was displeased with him; but Abel worshipped God, and was loved by him, which caused Cain to rise up and kill his brother Abel.

Ques. What should this teach us?
Ans. To worship God sincerely.
Ques. What shall we call Cain?
Ans. The first murderer.
Ques. What shall we call Abel?
Ans. The first martyr.
Ques. Why shall we call him a martyr?
Ans. Because he was killed for his love to God.
Ques. Have any, since Abel, been killed for loving and serving God?

Ans. Yes, very many; Stephen was stoned to death.
Ques. What did the Lord say to Cain after he had killed his brother?
Ans. Where is Abel, thy brother?
Ques. What was Cain's reply?
Ans. I know not. Am I my brother's keeper?
Ques. What did the Lord then say?
Ans. What hast thou done.
Ques. What cried to the Lord from the ground?
Ans. The blood of Abel.
Ques. How did the Lord punish Cain?
Ans. He drove him away from his friends.
Ques. What did he say Cain should be?
Ans. A vagabond and a fugitive in the earth.
Ques. What did he mean by this?
Ans. That he should not live in peace with **his friends**, **or** be loved by God.
Ques. How did he feel?
Ans. Very bad indeed.
Ques. What did he say?
Ans. My punishment is greater than I can bear.
Ques. What was Cain afraid of?
Ans. That he should be killed.
Ques. Why was Cain afraid of being killed?
Ans. Because it was known that he killed Abel.
Ques. Do wicked people do many things that they would not do if they knew they should be found out?
Ans. They do; but God always sees them.

Teacher. Yes, my little children, God always sees you, and knows when you are doing something that you would not do if you knew some one saw you.

Ques. Where did Cain go?
Ans. He went out from the east of Eden.
Ques. What did he become?
Ans. A vagabond.
Ques. Do you think Cain was happy?

Ans. We do not, for he was not loved.
Ques. What will make us loved?
Ans. Good behavior.
Ques. Was Cain guilty of any other sins but murder?
Ans. He was.
Ques Name them.
Ans. 1st. He did not worship God as he should. 2d. He hated Abel because he was good. 3d. After he had killed him, he told a wicked lie to hide his sin.
Ques. Do wicked children ever tell a lie to hide their sins?
Ans. They do.
Ques. Who is the father of lies?
Ans. The wicked spirit that told an untruth to Eve.
Ques. You see that Eve's son was a murderer and a liar; was God's image on his soul?
Ans. It was not.

> "By envious Cain we're taught
>   How murder may begin,
> And how one angry, jealous thought
>   May lead to greater sin.

> "Our evil actions spring
>   From small and hidden seeds;
> At first we think some wicked thing,
>   Then practise wicked deeds.

> "Cain once, perhaps, might start
>   At what he soon would be;
> But they that trust an evil heart,
>   May prove as vile as he."

LESSON XVII.

THE FLOOD.

Ques. Little children, you have learned that the world became wicked. Did it grow any better after a great many years?
Ans. It did not.
Ques. When the Lord saw the wickedness of men, how did he feel?
Ans. It grieved him.
Ques. What did he resolve to do?
Ans. To drown the world.
Ques. What is it to drown?
Ans. To cover all over with water.
Ques. If the world was drowned, what was to become of the people?
Ans. They would all die.
Ques. Did any one know that God was going to drown the world?

Ans. He told a good man, named Noah.
Ques. What does the Bible say about him?
Ans. That he was a just and perfect man.
Ques. How many sons had he?
Ans. Three.
Ques. What are their names?
Ans. Ham, Shem, and Japhet.
Ques. What did the Lord say to Noah after he had told him that he would drown the world?
Ans. Make thee an ark.
Ques. What was the ark like?
Ans. Like a large ship with a roof on it.
Ques. Did Noah know how to make an ark?
Ans. He did not, but God told him how.
Ques. What did the Lord say to Noah after the ark was made?
Ans. Thou shalt come into the ark.
Ques. Who did he command him to take into the ark with him?
Ans. His three sons and their wives.
Ques. What were they to bring into the ark with them?
Ans. Cattle, fowls, and creeping things.
Ques. How many?
Ans. Two of a kind.
Ques. Why were they to take them into the ark?
Ans. To keep them alive.
Ques. How many persons were saved in the ark?
Ans. Eight.
Ques. Who were they?
Ans. Noah and his wife, his sons and their wives.
Ques. Who shut them into the ark?
Ans. God.

"When the great and mighty flood
Came upon a world of sin,
Noah made an ark of wood,
God was pleased to shut him in."

Ques. How long did it rain?
Ans. Forty days and forty nights.
Ques. How long did the water cover the earth?
Ans. One hundred and fifty days.
Ques. How long before the ground was dry enough for Noah to till it?
Ans. Three hundred and sixty-five days.
Ques. How much does that make?
Ans. One spring and summer, one fall and winter.
Ques. What does that make?
Ans. One year.
Ques. What had become of all the wicked people, and cattle?
Ans. They were all dead.
Ques. Could not some of them have climbed up on some high mountain and been kept alive?
Ans. They could not; for every high hill and mountain was covered.

> " When the dark and heavy cloud
> Lifts on high its awful form,
> And above us, pealing loud,
> Rolls the thunder of the storm,
> Do not fear the lightning's flash,
> God directs it where to fall;
> Do not fear the thunder's crash,
> For your Saviour rules them all."

LESSON XVIII.

THE FLOOD — CONTINUED.

Ques. The world was drowned because of wickedness. What should this teach us?
Ans. That God will destroy sinners.
Ques. Noah was a good man, and God saved him in the ark. What should this teach us?

Ans. That God cares for good people.
Ques. Did the ark float along upon the water as ships do?
Ans. It did.

> "There was a lonely ark,
>   That sailed o'er waters dark;
> And, wide around,
> Not one tall tree was seen,
> Nor flower, nor leaf of green:
>   All, all were drowned."

Ques. Where did it rest, when the water began to go down?
Ans. On a mountain.
Ques. What is a mountain?
Ans. A very high hill.
Ques. What was the name of the mountain upon which the ark rested?
Ans. Ararat.
Ques. When Noah saw the waters drying up, what did he do?
Ans. He sent out a raven.
Ques. What is a raven?
Ans. A large blackbird.
Ques. Was the raven taken into the ark again?
Ans. It was not.
Ques. What other bird did he send out seven days after?
Ans. A dove.

> "Then a soft wing was spread,
>   And o'er the billows dread
>   A meek dove flew;
> But on that shoreless tide
> No living thing she spied,
>   To cheer her view."

Ques. What did the dove do?
Ans. It came back to the ark; for the water covered the earth.

Ques. How long did Noah wait before he again sent he dove to see if the water had dried up?
Ans. Seven days.
Ques. What did the dove do?
Ans. It came back to the ark with an olive leaf in its mouth.

> "So to the ark she fled,
> With weary, drooping head,
>   To seek for rest:
> Christ is THY ark, my love,
> Thou art the timid dove —
>   Fly to his breast."

Ques. After seven other days, Noah sent out the dove again, and it did not come back; then he knew that the water was gone from the earth. What did he do?
Ans. He took the covering off the ark.
Ques. Who spoke to him, and told him to go out from the ark?
Ans. God.
Ques. How long had he been in the ark?
Ans. One year.
Ques. What did Noah do soon after he left the ark?
Ans. He built an altar, and offered burnt sacrifice.
Ques. What is a burnt-offering?
Ans. A lamb, or any clean beast, entirely burnt as a sacrifice to God.
Ques. What did a burnt sacrifice show?
Ans. That their lives could have been justly taken, and their souls deserved eternal fire.
Ques. Was God pleased with Noah when he sacrificed to him?
Ans. He was, and said, I will not again curse the ground, for man's sake.
Ques. What did he say of seed-time and harvest?
Ans. They shall never cease.
Ques. What of summer and winter, and of day and night?
Ans. They shall never stop.

Ques. What did he make with Noah and his sons?
Ans. A promise that he would never more drown the world.
Ques. What did he give him for a sign?
Ans. He set the beautiful rainbow in the sky.

LESSON XIX.

NOAH AFTER THE FLOOD, AND STRONG DRINK.

Ques. How long did Noah live after the flood?
Ans. Three hundred and fifty years.
Ques. How long did he live before the flood?
Ans. Six hundred years.
Ques. Noah was a very old man; do you know of one that lived more years than Noah?
Ans. Methuselah did.
Ques. How old was Methuselah?
Ans. Nine hundred and sixty-nine.
Ques. Did he live before or after the flood?
Ans. Before the flood.
Ques. Did Noah live in a house as we do?
Ans. He did not; he lived in a tent.
Ques. What did he do after he made his tent?
Ans. He went to farming.
Ques. What did he plant?
Ans. A vineyard.
Ques. What grew in a vineyard?
Ans. Grapes.
Ques. What is made of grapes?
Ans. Wine.
Ques. What will wine make of people who drink too much of it?
Ans. Drunkards.

Ques. Did Noah drink wine?
Ans. He did.
Ques. What did it do to him?
Ans. It made him drunken.
Ques. Is it probable that Noah knew that it would make him drunken?
Ans. It is not.
Ques. Will good men drink wine and strong drink?
Ans. They will not.
Ques. What does the Bible say of wine?
Ans. Wine is a mocker.
Ques. What of strong drink?
Ans. Strong drink is raging.
Ques. What is strong drink?
Ans. Brandy, rum, gin, wine, cider, and strong beer.
Ques. What does the Bible say of those that are deceived by it?
Ans. They are not wise.
Ques. What does the Bible say of drunkards?
Ans. No drunkard shall enter the kingdom of heaven.
Ques. What do they have that tarry long at the wine?
Ans. Woe, sorrow quarrellings, vain talk, and red eyes.
Ques. What does the wisest man say it biteth like?
Ans. It biteth like a serpent.
Ques. What is a serpent?
Ans. A large snake.
Ques. How do they bite?
Ans. Very slily.
Ques. What is said of the sting of wine?
Ans. It stingeth like an adder.
Ques. What is an adder?
Ans. A very poisonous snake.
Ques. Then if wine and strong drink biteth and stingeth like a snake, what should it teach us?
Ans. To let it alone, and never taste it.

"I seek for blessings more divine
Than corn or oil or richest wine;
If these are sent, I 'll praise my God;
Withheld, still sound his praise abroad.

"One thing I ask, and wilt thou hear,
And grant my soul a gift so dear?
Wisdom descending from above;
The choicest token of thy love.

"Wisdom, betimes to know the Lord,
To fear his name, and keep his word;
To lead my feet in paths of truth,
And guide and guard my wandering youth."

LESSON XX.

BABEL, AND THE PEOPLE SCATTERED.

After a number of hundred years there was a great number of people upon the earth, and they lived together on a plain called Shinar.

Ques. On what plain did they live?
Ans. The plain of Shinar.
Ques. What kind of country is a plain?
Ans. A level country with no hills.
Ques. What did they say one to another?
Ans. Let us make bricks, and build a city and a tower.
Ques. What is a tower?
Ans. A very high house.
Ques. Why did they wish to build this city?
Ans. So as to live together, and have one ruler.
Ques. What is a ruler?
Ans. In some countries, kings, and others, presidents
Ques. Which do we have?
Ans. Presidents.
Ques. Of what were they going to build the city?

Ans. Of bricks and slime.
Ques. How high did they propose to build the **tower?**
Ans. As high as the heavens.
Ques. Did this please the Lord?
Ans. It did not, for he did not like to have them all ive in one place.
Ques. What did he do?
Ans. He confused them.
Ques. How did he confuse them?
Ans. He caused them to speak in different languages
Ques. Had they all talked alike before this?
Ans. They had.
Ques. What did they do when they could not undertand each other?
Ans. They stopped building the tower, and some vent to one place and others went to other places.
Ques. Do people all speak alike now?
Ans. They do not.
Ques. What is the place called where God confounded ind scattered the people?
Ans. Babel.
Ques. Do all people worship the same God now?
Ans. They do not. Some worship idols.
Ques. What are idols that some worship?
Ans. Images made of wood and stones.
Ques. What do others worship?
Ans. Sun, moon, and stars.

I shall not ask you any thing more about those that do iot worship the God of heaven now, as I intend to hereifter.

Ques. Will you tell me if the people who built Babel iad a Bible to tell them what was God's will?
Ans. They had not.
Ques. How, then, did they know his will?
Ans. He talked with good men and told them what hey must do, and they told all the people.

Ques. What do some think the people were going to do in the tower of Babel?
Ans. Worship idols.

> "I thank the goodness and the grace
> Which on my birth have smiled,
> And made me, in these Christian days,
> A free and happy child.
>
> "I was not born, as thousands are,
> Where God was never known;
> And taught to pray a useless prayer
> To blocks of wood and stone.
>
> "I was not born without a home,
> Or in some broken shed,
> A gipsy baby taught to roam,
> And steal my daily bread.
>
> "My God, I thank thee, who hast planned
> A better lot for me,
> And placed me in this happy land,
> Where I may hear of thee."

LESSON XXI.

THE COMMANDMENTS, AND HOW GIVEN.

We have learned how God scattered the people, so that they lived all over a great many countries. Now I wish to tell you that there were some people, called Israelites, that God loved more than he did the rest, and he called them his people, and wished to have them obey him; so he chose the meekest man to be their ruler; and he used to talk with him and tell him how to govern this great nation.

Ques. What was this people called?
Ans. Israelites.
Ques. What was the name of their Ruler?

Ans. Moses.
Ques. What is Moses called?
Ans. The meekest man.
Ques. What did the Lord say to Moses one day as he went up Mount Sinai?
Ans. If this people will obey me, then shall they be my people.
Ques. What did they say when Moses told them this?
Ans. We will do all the Lord hath spoken.
Ques. What was heard three days after this?
Ans. Thunders, and the sound of a trumpet.
Ques. What was on the mountain?
Ans. A black cloud, and lightnings.
Ques. How did all the people feel when they heard the thunders and the trumpet, and saw the lightning and dark clouds?
Ans. They trembled and were afraid.
Ques. What did Moses do?
Ans. He led the people to the foot of the mountain to meet God.
Ques. What was then done?
Ans. The Lord came down upon the mountain, and Moses went up to him.
Ques. How long did Moses stay upon the mountain?
Ans. Forty days.
Ques. What did the Lord give to him?
Ans. Two tables of stone.
Ques. What was written on them?
Ans. Ten commandments.
Ques. Who gave the commandments to Moses?
Ans. The Lord God.
Ques. The commandments are very long, but I have them in verse. Will you repeat the first two, and so on
Ans.

    1st. Thou no gods shalt have but me;
    2d. Before no idol bow thy knee;
    3d. Take not the name of God in vain;

4th. Dare not the Sabbath day profane.
5th. Give both thy parents honor due;
6th. Take heed that thou no murder do;
7th. Abstain from words and deeds unclean;
8th. Steal not, though thou be poor and mean,
9th. Make not a wilful lie, nor love it;
10th. What is thy neighbor's dare not covet.

Ques. Should we obey these commands?
Ans. We must, and then God will be pleased with us.
Ques. What if we do not obey them?
Ans. He will be angry with us.
Ques. When were they written?
Ans. A great many hundred years ago.
Ques. In view of keeping the commands, what should be our prayer?
Ans

"Jesus, high in glory,
  Lend a listening ear;
When we bow before thee,
  Infant praises hear.

"We are little children,
  Weak, and apt to stray;
Saviour, guide and keep us
  In the heavenly way.

"Keep us, Lord, from sinning,
  Watch us day by day;
Help us now to love thee,
  Take our sins away.

"Then, when Jesus calls us
  To our heavenly home,
We will gladly answer,
  Saviour, Lord, I come."

LESSON XXII.

IDOLATRY AND PRAYER.

Ques. Little children, if I should love and think more about you than any thing besides, what should I be called?

Ans. An idolater.

Ques. If you love your doll or rocking-horse more than God, what shall we call you?

Ans. An idolater.

Ques. What is an idolater?

Ans. It is one who loves some object or thing more than God.

Ques. We should love and obey our parents and teachers, but who should we love more?

Ans. God.

Ques. To whom should we pray?

Ans. To God.

"God is in heaven; and can he hear
A feeble prayer like mine?
Yes, little child, thou need'st not fear,
He listens now to thine."

Ques. What is prayer?
Ans.

"Prayer is the simplest form of speech
That infant lips can try;
Prayer, the sublimest strains that reach
The majesty on high.

"Prayer is the Christian's vital breath,
The Christian's native air;
His watchword at the gates of death,
He enters heaven with prayer."

Ques. Some little children kneel and pray to pictures and images. Is this right?

Ans. It is not.

Ques. What does the Bible say about it?
Ans. Thou shalt not bow down to them, nor serve them.
Ques. Some pray to good people that have died do you think that they can bless them?
Ans. We do not.
Ques. Why not?
Ans. Because they cannot bless themselves.
Ques. Who can bless every one?
Ans. God.
Ques. To whom does the Bible say we should pray?
Ans. To our father in heaven, who seeth in secret.
Ques. Why should we pray to him?
Ans. Because he has said, Ask, and ye shall receive.
Ques What does St. Paul say?
Ans. Pray without ceasing.

"What is an idol? Every breast
Has idols of its own;
Sometimes of gold and silver bright,
Sometimes of wood and stone.

"And these are idols — sins, I mean —
Which young and old adore;
O, God of mercy! in thy love
Destroy them evermore.

"If there be aught the world contains
Which I love more than thee,
That sinful love within my heart
Idolatry must be.

"Then take that sinful love away,
And place thy love within;
And break down every image there,
That bears the shape of sin.

"Deeply inscribed on my heart,
Let thy commandments be;
That there may live within my breast
None other God but thee."

LESSON XXIII.

IDOLATRY AND HEATHENISM.

Ques. There are a great many people and children that have images of the sun and moon, and of crocodiles and other creatures, which they worship as God. What do we call them?

Ans. Heathen.

Ques. Are the heathens afraid of their gods?

Ans. They are.

Ques. Why are they?

Ans. Because they think they make them sick and die.

Ques. What do they do to make peace with their gods?

Ans. They make presents to them.

Ques. Can you tell me the name of a river that the Hindoos worship?

Ans. Ganges.

Ques. What live in this river?

Ans. Crocodiles.

Ques. What are crocodiles?

Ans. A large animal that has great teeth, and could bite us in two with them.

Ques. What do the Hindoos think of them?

Ans. That they are gods.

Ques. What do they throw to these dreadful creatures?

Ans. Little children.

Ques. What do we call these poor, ignorant people?

Ans. Heathens.

Ques. Why do they give their little children to these dreadful creatures?

Ans. Because they think it will please them.

Ques. Are the heathen idolaters then?

Ans. They are, but they do not know about the true God.

Ques. Are the idolaters you told me about in your last lesson, heathen?

Ans. They are not, because they knew about the true God.

Ques. Which do you think are the worst, idolaters in heathen countries or idolaters in Christian countries?

Ans. Those in Christian countries.

Ques. Is ours a Christian country?

Ans. It is, for we have the Bible, and ministers to preach to us.

Ques. How should we feel towards the heathen?

Ans. We should pity and pray for them.

Ques. Have we heathen in our town?

Ans. We have not.

Ques. Have we idolaters in the town?

Ans. We think we have.

Ques. Describe some that you think are idolaters?

Ans. 1st. All that think more of fine clothes than of God. Also, 2d. Those that think more of money than of God. 3d. All that think more of fine rides than of God. 4th. All that think more of themselves than of God.

Ques. Where are heathen to be found?

Ans. In countries where they have no Bible to read.

Ques. Where are idolaters to be found?

Ans. In all countries.

> "Poor little heathen boy,
>   How sad I feel for thee;
> Your ears have never heard
>   What mother tells to me.
>
> "She tells me of a God,
>   That made both you and me,
> To whom we oft should bow
>   Upon the bended knee.
>
> "He is both great and wise;
>   He gives us all our food;

And loves us when we try
To serve him, and be good.

"When I am older grown.
I then will tell you more,
For mother bids me go
To your benighted shore;

"And tell you all about
The Saviour and his love,
That you may love him too,
And dwell with him above."

LESSON XXIV.

ABOUT SWEARING.

Little children, you have heard much about **God's** holiness and greatness and goodness.

Ques. How should we speak of him?
Ans. Very carefully.
Ques. Should we call upon his name when we are playing and laughing?
Ans. We should not, nor when we are angry.
Ques. Should we ever call upon his name?
Ans. We should.
Ques. Why should we call upon his name?
Ans. 1st. To thank him for his goodness. 2d. To praise him for his mercies. 3d. To ask him to relieve us in the day of trouble. 4th. To ask him to forgive our sins.
Ques. What is it to swear?
Ans. To use the name of God in a wicked manner
Ques. What does the Bible say about it?
Ans. Take not the name of God in vain.
Ques. What is it to take his name in vain?
Ans. To call it in a careless manner

Ques. How should you feel if you should hear naughty children and wicked men calling your father's name for sport, or to threaten some one?
Ans. We should feel very bad.

Yes, my little children, you would feel bad if you knew that wicked men and boys used your father's name in a rude and careless manner. How much more should we feel sorry to hear them profaning our heavenly Father's name.

Ques. To what are swearers exposed?
Ans To God's wrath.
Ques. Should we be afraid of an angry God?
Ans. Yes!

> " How will they stand before his face,
> Who treated him with such disdain,
> While he shall doom them to the place
> Of everlasting fire and pain?"

Ques. What does Jesus Christ say about swearing?
Ans. Swear not at all.
Ques. Do you ever think that you will swear?
Ans. We think not.
Ques. It is wicked to swear. Do you think it is right to call each other names?
Ans.

> " Cross names and angry words require
> To be chastised at school;
> And he's in danger of hell-fire
> That calls his brother, fool."

Ques. I have heard men and children say, "God knows." What may this be called?
Ans. One kind of swearing.
Ques. Should we not be careful of all our words?
Ans. We should, for —

> " God is in heaven, and men below;
> Be short our tunes, our words be few:
> A solemn reverence checks our songs,
> And praise sits silent on our tongues."

Ques. Is it best for children to play with those that swear, and use bad language?
Ans. It is not.

"Why should I join with those in play,
In whom I 've no delight;
Who curse and swear, but never pray;
Who call ill names, and fight.

"Away from such I 'll turn my eyes,
Nor with the scoffers go;
I would be walking with the wise,
That wiser I might grow."

LESSON XXV.

HOW TO KEEP THE SABBATH.

"You must not play on Sunday, on Sunday;
But you may play on Monday, on Tuesday;
You may play on Wednesday, on Thursday, on Friday,
You may play on Saturday till Sunday comes again."

Ques. How many names have days?
Ans. Seven.
Ques. What are they?
Ans. Sunday, Monday, Tuesday, Wednesday, Thursday, Friday, and Saturday.
Ques. How many of these days are ours, to work in or play, just as we please?
Ans. Six.
Ques. Which day has God reserved for us to worship in, and rest from our work?
Ans. Sunday.
Ques. What should we do on Sunday?
Ans. We must worship God.
Ques. How do people worship God?
Ans. In thinking of him and praying to him, and singing praises to his name.
Ques. Is it right to do any thing more on Sunday?
Ans. We should learn about God and heaven.
Ques. Where do we go to hear about God?
Ans. To church and Sabbath school.
Ques. Then, if we learn about God in church and Sabbath school, should we stay away from the church and school?
Ans. We must not.
Ques. If we stay away from church, what are we likely to do?
Ans. To think and talk about vain things.
Ques. Whose day is the Sabbath?
Ans. God's day.
Ques. How does he say we must keep it?
Ans. Keep it holy.
Ques. Mention some things that little children do that break the Sabbath?
Ans. Play with kittens, look at their toys, and play with each other.
Ques. Tell me some things that 't is wrong to do on Sunday?

Ans.

"We must not work, we must not play,
Upon God's holy Sabbath day."

Ques. Can you name something that men do who break the Sabbath?

Ans. Walk about, and ride out for pleasure.

Ques. Shall I tell you a story about a man that broke the Sabbath when Moses ruled the people Israel?

A great many hundred years ago, when Moses ruled Israel, he told the people that they must not gather wood, etc., on Sunday, so they used to prepare their food and wood on Saturday. But there was a wicked man who saw some nice sticks of wood, and he thought what a nice fire they would make, and as he was alone he took them in his arms, and was carrying them home, when some men saw him, and made him throw down his wood, and took him to prison, and kept him there till Moses went and asked the Lord what they should do with this man for breaking the Sabbath.

Ques. And what do you think he told them?
Ans. To stone him till he died.

Yes, they took him out of prison and threw stones upon him till he died.

Ques. If God commanded them to stone that man to death for getting wood on Sunday, do you not think he will punish us if we break the Sabbath?

Ans. We do.

"This day belongs to God alone,
This day he chooses for his own,
And we must neither work nor play,
Because it is God's holy day.

'We ought, to-day, to learn and seek
What we may think of all the week,
And be the better every day
For what we hear our teachers say."

LESSON XXVI.

OBEDIENCE TO PARENTS.

Ques. How should you feel towards your parents?
Ans. Love them.
Ques. If you love them, how will you behave to them?
Ans. Obey them, and try to please them.
Ques. Suppose you want something very much, which your parents think you should not have; how will you behave then?
Ans. We shall say, "I should like it; but if you wish me not to have it, I will go without it."
Ques. But if children are naughty, and do not love their parents as they should, how will they behave when they are told not to touch any thing?
Ans. They will cry, and try to get it.

Ques. Did you ever see a boy or girl do so?
Teach. If you did, you saw a naughty child.
Ques. If you love your parents, you will obey them; but I have seen some children obey their parents, and look very sour about it. Did they obey because they loved to?
Ans. We should think not.
Ques. What do you think made them obey?
Ans. They were afraid of being punished.
Ques. If children love their parents, will they fear them?
Ans. They will fear to make them unhappy.
Ques. How will good children feel when they make their parents unhappy?
Ans. They will be sorry, and ask them to forgive them.
Ques. Should children ever speak an angry word, or look ugly to their parents?
Ans. He that curseth or smiteth his father or mother shall be put to death.
Ques. What is it to smite?
Ans. To strike.
Ques. What is it to curse?
Ans. To speak wicked and angry words.
Ques. Should parents punish a bad child?
Ans. They should not spare the rod for his much crying.
Ques. What does the Bible say will spoil a child?
Ans. To spare the rod.
Ques. Will a good parent neglect to punish a child when it has done wrong?
Ans. We think not; for the Bible commands him to correct those that obey not.
Ques. What does the Bible say to children about obeying their parents?
Ans. Children, obey your parents in the Lord, for this is right.

Ques. What is promised to good and obedient children?

Ans. Long and happy lives.

Ques. What kind of words should you give to your parents?

Ans. Pleasant words.

Ques. If your parents are wicked, what is your duty to them?

Ans. Love them, respect them, obey them.

> "O that it were my chief delight
> To do the things I ought!
> Then let me try with all my might
> To mind what I am taught.
>
> "Whenever I am told to go,
> I 'll cheerfully obey;
> Nor will I mind it much, although
> I leave a pretty play.
>
> "When I am bid I 'll freely bring
> Whatever I have got,
> And never touch a pretty thing,
> If mother tells me not.
>
> "When she permits me, I may tell
> About my little toys;
> But if she 's busy or unwell,
> I must not make a noise.
>
> "And when I learn my hymns to say
> And work and read and spell,
> I will not think about my play,
> But try to do it well."

LESSON XXVII.

LYING AND STEALING.

Repeat in concert —

"Make not a wilful lie, nor love it;
What is thy neighbor's, dare not covet."

Ques. Where is this written?
Ans. In the commandments.
Ques. What is it to tell a lie?
Ans. To tell something that is not true.
Ques. How are liars regarded?
Ans.

"Abhorred of men the liar shall be;
None can a liar trust;
His name is stained with infamy,
And trampled in the dust."

Now suppose your mother has forbidden you to touch the fruit that is in the dish, and you take an apple. She sees it is gone, and says, " Have you taken an apple from the dish ?" and you should say " No."

Ques. Would this be telling the truth ?
Ans. It would not ; it would be telling a lie.

Once a little sick girl had a penny, which she wanted her brother to take and buy some lemon drops for her He went and purchased them, and going home he thought how nice they were, and wished they were his; so he opened the paper, and began to eat them ; and they were so good he ate them up, and told his sister that he had dropped the penny, and so she went without any lemon drops.

Ques. What did this boy do ?
Ans. He made a lie, and told it.
Ques. Of what was the boy guilty before telling the lie ?
Ans. Of wishing for something that did not belong to him.
Ques. What is that called ?
Ans. Coveting.
Ques. Is that forbidden ?
Ans. Thou shalt not covet, is a command
Ques. Was the boy guilty of something besides coveting and lying ?
Ans He took and ate something that did not belong to him.
Ques. What is taking what does not belong to you called ?
Ans. Stealing.
Ques. Is this forbidden too ?
Ans Thou shalt not steal, is one of the commandments.

Ques. What did a good man say about stealing?
Ans.
> "It is a sin
> To steal a pin;
> Much more to steal
> A greater thing."

Ques. When any one steals, do they expect to be seen?
Ans. They do not.
Ques. Who does see them?
Ans. The all-seeing God.
Ques. If no one sees them will they be punished?
Ans. They will when they die, unless they repent and ask to be forgiven.
Ques. Will they be punished here if they are found out?
Ans. Most certainly.

> "Great God! and since thy piercing eye
> My inmost heart can see,
> Teach me from every sin to fly,
> And turn my heart to thee."

Ques. How many things was this boy guilty of?
Ans. Coveting, stealing, and lying.

> "The Lord abhors a lying tongue,
> Addicted to defame;
> He sees the base deceit and wrong,
> And brings the wretch to shame.

> "He will the guilty liar shake,
> In his most dreadful ire;
> And fix his portion in the lake
> Of everlasting fire."

LESSON XXVIII

LYING — CONTINUED.

"I must not lie,
 I must not feign,
 I must not take
   God's name in vain."

Ques. Now, little boys and girls, you have often been told that it is wicked to tell a lie. But I am afraid that many children deny the truth. Sometimes because they have done some mischief, and wish to escape punishment; so they say they did not do it. Do they speak the truth?

Ans. That is denying the truth.

Ques. Is that right?

Ans. It is not; it is just as wicked as telling a lie.

Ques. What is it to deny the truth?

Ans. One way of lying.

Ques. What is it to tell a story that we know is not true, because we have heard some one else tell the story?

Ans. It is reporting a lie.

Ques. What is it to make a story and tell it?

Ans. It is making a lie.

Ques. I wish you to learn what the Lord says about lying.

Ans. 1st. Put away lying. 2d. Speak every man truth with his neighbor. 3d. Lie not one to another

Ques. What does the Lord hate?

Ans. A proud look and a lying tongue.

Ques. What is an abomination to the Lord?

Ans. Lying lips.

"Have we not known nor heard nor read,
 How God abhors deceit and wrong?"

Ques. Children, can you tell me who was struck dead for lying?

Ans. A man named Ananias, and his wife Sapphira.

Ques. What should this teach us?

Ans. To be careful, and speak the truth.

Ques. Why do wicked people lie?

Ans. To hide their faults.

Ques. If we have done wrong, which is best, to confess our wrong, or to hide it with a lie?

Ans. To confess our wrongs.

> " God made our eyes, and can discern
> Whichever way we think to turn:
> In every place, by night or day,
> He watches all we do or say."

Ques. What will become of liars?

Ans. All liars shall have their part in the lake that burneth with fire and brimstone.

Ques. Should any of you like to have a part in that lake?

Ans. Oh no! It would be dreadful indeed.

Ques. How long will the fire burn in the lake?

Ans. Forever and ever.

Ques. How should good boys and girls always act?

Ans.

> " Good boys and girls should always try
> To act as shall not need a lie;
> But cheerful, innocent, and gay,
> As passes by the smiling day,
> You 'll never have to turn aside
> From any one, your faults to hide."

CHILD'S BIBLE

LESSON XXIX.

WHAT IS IT TO BREAK THE COMMANDMENTS?

> "There is a land above,
>   All beautiful and bright;
> And those that love the Lord
>   Rise to that world of light
>
> "There sin is known no more,
>   Nor tears nor want nor care;
> There good and happy spirits dwell,
>   And all are holy there."

Ques. Do you think that any one who breaks the commandments will go to the happy land that we have just sung about?

Ans. We do not; for

> "God requires a strict account
>   Of all the works they do."

Ques. What is it to break the first command?
Ans. To love something or some one more than God

Ques. What is that called?
Ans. Idolatry.
Ques. How is the second command broken?
Ans. In kneeling and praying to idols and saints.
Ques. What is it to break the third command?
Ans. To speak of God carelessly.
Ques. What is that called?
Ans. Swearing.
Ques. What is it to break the fourth command?
Ans. To play or work on Sunday.
Ques. What are those called that break the Sabbath?
Ans. Sabbath-breakers.
Ques. How is the fifth command broken?
Ans. By being unkind, and disobeying parents.
Ques. How is the sixth command broken?
Ans. By getting angry, and wishing some one dead.

I have heard very wicked children say, "I wish you was dead," to their little mates. Now this was very wicked indeed; and if these children do not reform, I am afraid they will kill some one when they get older.

Ques. If they should, what would they be called?
Ans. Murderers.
Ques. What is said of murderers?
Ans. No murderer can enter heaven
Ques. How is the seventh command broken?
Ans. By using vulgar and bad words.
Ques. How is the eighth command broken?
Ans. In slyly taking something that is not yours.
Ques. What is that called?
Ans. Stealing.
Ques. How is the ninth command broken?
Ans. In telling or making a lie; in deceiving, and in denying the truth.
Ques. How is the ninth command broken?
Ans. By wishing very much for something that is an-

Ques. What is this called?
Ans. Coveting.

[In the order above, I have numbered the commandments as they are in verse, omitting the last one in the text.]

Ques. What rests upon those that break the commandments?
Ans. God's curse.
Ques. What rests upon those that keep them?
Ans. His blessing.
Ques. What is said of those that keep the commandments?
Ans. They shall fear no evil.
Ques. Who will love us if we are good?
Ans. God, and the angels, and good people.
Ques. How shall we feel to have God and angels love us?
Ans. Very happy.

> "Make me to walk in thy commands,
> 'T is a delightful road;
> Nor let my head nor heart nor hands
> Offend against my God."

LESSON XXX.

REVIEW.

Ques. Name of the first man?
Ans. Adam.
Ques. Name of the first woman?
Ans. Eve.
Ques. Who was the first murderer?
Ans. Cain.

Ques. Name the first martyr?
Ans. Abel.
Ques. What is a martyr?
Ans. One that is killed because he loves God.
Ques. How was Cain punished for killing his brother?
Ans. He was driven from his friends.
Ques. What did Cain do after he killed his brother?
Ans. He told a wicked lie to cover his sin.
Ques. Who is the father of lies?
Ans. The old serpent that lied to Eve.

"Lo, God is in heaven, and would he know
If I should tell a lie?"

Teacher.

"Yes, if thou said it ever so low,
He'd hear it in the sky."

Ques. Can you tell me who was saved in the ark when the world was drowned?
Ans. Noah and his wife, his three sons and their wives.
Ques. Why was the world drowned?
Ans. Because it was so wicked.
Ques. Was Noah a good man?
Ans. He was.
Ques. What was saved in the ark with Noah and his family?
Ans. Cattle and beasts and birds, two of every kind.
Ques. How long did it rain?
Ans. Forty days and forty nights.
Ques. How long was Noah in the ark?
Ans. One year.
Ques. When the ark stopped floating, where did it rest?
Ans. Mount Ararat.
Ques. What did Noah send out of the ark to see if the water was gone off the ground?
Ans. A raven, and, after seven days, a little dove.

Ques. When the dove did not return to the ark, what did Noah think?

Ans. That the waters had gone off the ground.

Ques. What did he then do?

Ans. He, and all that were with him, went out of the ark.

Ques. What did Noah do when he was come out of the ark?

Ans. He built an altar, and worshipped God.

Ques. What did he do after he had built an house to live in?

Ans. He tilled the ground.

Ques. What do we call a tiller of the ground?

Ans. A farmer.

Ques. Was God pleased with Noah?

Ans. He was, because he built an altar and gave thanks to God.

Ques. What should this teach us?

Ans. To commence the day and New Year with prayer and praise.

Ques. What did God make with Noah and his sons?

Ans. A covenant.

Ques. What was the covenant?

Ans. That he would never drown the world again.

Ques. What sign did he give him?

Ans. The rainbow.

Ques. How long did Noah live after the flood?

Ans. Three hundred and fifty years.

Ques. By this time there were a great many people on the earth, but they were not scattered all abroad as they are now, and did not wish to be. What did they resolve to build?

Ans. A great city, with a high tower in it.

Ques. Did this please the Lord?

Ans. It did not.

Ques. What did he do?

Ans. He confounded their language, so that they could not understand each other.
Ques. Did they finish the tower?
Ans. They did not, they were scattered all abroad.
Ques. Do people live all over the earth now?
Ans. They do.
Ques. Do all worship the same God?
Ans. They do not. Some worship idols.

LESSON XXXI.

REVIEW.

Ques. How many commandments are there?
Ans. Ten.
Ques. Upon what were they written?
Ans. Upon tables of stone.
Ques. Who wrote them?
Ans. God.
Ques. Can you repeat the commandments in poetry? See 21st lesson.
Ques. Where did Moses go for the commandments?
Ans. Mount Sinai.
Ques. What was the appearance of the mountain?
Ans. It trembled, and smoke went up from all around it.
Ques. What was heard upon the mountain?
Ans. The sound of a trumpet.
Ques. When the sound became louder and louder, what did Moses do?
Ans. He spoke, and God answered him by a voice.
Ques. How did the people feel?
Ans. They were afraid, and trembled.
Ques. Did any go up on the mount but Moses?

Ans. They did not, for God commanded that they should not touch it.

Ques. How should we regard the commands?

Ans. With sacred awe.

Ques. Should we dare to disobey them?

Ans. We should not.

Ques. Who are idolaters?

Ans. Those who love some other object more than God.

Ques. Is it wicked to pray to images and saints?

Ans. It is, for it breaks the second commandment.

Ques. Describe an idolater?

Ans. One who thinks more of fine clothes, nice rides, parties, money, and of themselves, than God.

Ques. What does the Bible say about using the name of God?

Ans. Take not his name in vain.

Ques. What is it to take his name in vain?

Ans. To use it in a laughing, careless manner.

Ques. How should we speak of God?

Ans. With respect.

Ques. Is it right to say "God knows," when we are talking?

Ans. It is not; it is a kind of swearing.

Ques. Where do we hear the most about God?

Ans. In church and Sunday school.

Ques. Will you tell me some things that it is wrong to do on Sunday?

Ans. We must not work or play on Sunday.

Ques. How can we keep the day holy?

Ans. By praying, reading good books, and going to church and Sunday school.

Ques. What does the Bible say about Sabbath day?

Ans. Remember the Sabbath day to keep it holy

Ques. What does the Bible say about obeying your parents?

Ans. Children, obey your parents in the Lord, for this is right.

Ques. What is promised to good and obedient children?

Ans. Long and happy lives.

Ques. What is it to covet?

Ans. To wish for something which belongs to some one else.

Ques. What does the Bible say about coveting?

Ans. Thou shalt not covet.

Ques. What is it to steal?

Ans. To take that which is not yours.

Ques. What is said about stealing in the Bible?

Ans. Thou shalt not steal.

Ques. When any one steals, do they expect to be seen?

Ans. They do not.

Ques. Will you repeat the little verse about stealing?

Ans.
"It is a sin
To steal a pin,
Much more to steal
A greater thing."

Ques. Will you say the one about lying?

Ans.
"I must not tell a lie,
I must not feign,
I must not take
God's name in vain."

Ques. Tell me what God says about lying.

Ans. Put away lying; speak every man the truth with his neighbor.

Ques. What is an abomination to the Lord?

Ans. Lying lips.

LESSON XXXII.

THE BIRTH OF JESUS CHRIST.

"Hail thou blest morn, when the great Mediator
    Down from the regions of glory descend
Shepherds, go worship the babe in the manger;
    Lo, for his guide the bright angels attend.

"Brightest and best of the sons of the morning,
    Shine on our darkness, and lend us thine aid;
Star in the east, the horizon adorning,
    Guide where our infant Redeemer was laid."

Some time ago I told you that sin came into the world through disobedience, and that God gave a promise of mercy.

Ques. Can any of you tell what this promise was?
Ans. That his son should come into the world and save it from sin.
Teacher. Yes. God promised that his son Jesus Christ should leave his home in bright glory, and come into this sinful world and be put to death, that we might live in glory.
Ques. Can you tell me where he was to be born?
Ans. In Bethlehem of Judea.
Ques. Where did they lay him?
Ans In a manger.
Ques. What is a manger?
Ans. A stable where cattle feed.
Ques. Why did they lay him there?
Ans. Because there was no room in the house.
Ques. What was his mother's name?
Ans. Mary.
Ques What was her husband's name?
Ans. Joseph.
Ques. Who were in the country watching sheep?
Ans Men called shepherds.

Ques. Who came to these shepherds in the night as they were watching their sheep?
Ans. An angel of the Lord.
Ques. How did the shepherds feel?
Ans. They were afraid.
Ques. What did the angel say to them?
Ans. Fear not.
Ques. What did they bring to them?
Ans. Good tidings.
Ques. What was the good news?
Ans. That a Saviour was born.
Ques. What did they call him?
Ans. Christ, the Lord.
Ques. Where did the angels say they should find him?
Ans. In a manger.
Ques. What did the shepherds hear while the angels were talking?
Ans. A great many angels praising God.
Ques. What did the angels say?
Ans. Glory to God in the highest; on earth peace; good-will towards men.
Ques. What did the shepherds do when the angels were gone?
Ans. They went to Bethlehem to find the infant Saviour.
Ques. Did they find him?
Ans. They did.
Ques. What did they do when they had found him?
Ans. They worshipped him.
Ques. Did they tell what they had heard and seen?
Ans. They told Mary and others.
Ques. After the shepherds had seen the Saviour, what did they do?
Ans. They went back praising God.

LESSON XXXIII.

THE INFANT JESUS.

"Glory to God, that reigns above,
That pitied us forlorn;
We join to sing our Maker's love,
For there's a Saviour born."

Ques. Who told Mary what to call her son?
Ans. An angel.
Ques. How old was he when a name was given him?
Ans. Eight days old.
Ques. What did they call him?
Ans. Jesus.
Ques. Why was he called Jesus?
Ans. Because he was to save his people from their sins.
Ques. Where did his parents take him when he was forty days old?

Ans. Into the temple.
Ques. What is a temple?
Ans. A place of worship.
Ques. Who was in the temple when they went in with him?
Ans. A good man, called Simeon.
Ques. What did he do to the child?
Ans. He took him in his arms, and blessed him.
Ques. What did he say that Jesus should be to the Gentiles?
Ans. A light.
Ques. And what should he be to his people Israel?
Ans. Their glory.
Ques. How did Simeon know this?
Ans. The Holy Spirit had told him so.
Ques. Who was in the temple with Simeon?
Ans. Anne, a prophetess.
Ques. What did they say of Jesus?
Ans. That he was to be the Saviour of the world.
Ques. Were all the people rejoiced because Christ had come?
Ans. Herod the king was not.
Ques. Why was he not pleased?
Ans. He was afraid that the people would have Jesus for their king.
Ques. What did he command some wicked men to do?
Ans. To kill all the little children.
Ques. Why did he kill all the children?
Ans. He thought that Jesus would be among them, and be killed too.
Ques. Where was Jesus?
Ans. In Egypt.
Ques. Why was he there?
Ans. God had told his parents what Herod would do, and told them to go there.
Ques. When did they go?
Ans. In the same night that God bid them.

Ques. What should this teach us?
Ans. To obey as soon as we are commanded.
Ques. How long did they stay there?
Ans. Till Herod died.
Ques. How old was Jesus at that time?
Ans. A little more than two years.
Ques. Where did they live after Herod died?
Ans. In Nazareth.
Ques. Who told them to live there?
Ans. God told them, when they slept and **dreamed**
Ques. Why did they dwell in Nazareth?
Ans. That Jesus might be called a Nazarene.
Ques. Who had said he should be called a **Nazarene?**
Ans. A prophet of the Lord.
Ques When did he say this?
Ans. A great many hundred years before

" Hosanna to the Son
 Of David and of God,
Who brought the news of pardon down,
And bought it with his blood."

QUESTION BOOK.

LESSON XXXIV.

SERMON ON THE MOUNT.

Ques. How old was Jesus when he began to preach?
Ans. About thirty years.
Ques. Did he preach in one place all the time?
Ans. He did not; he went from place to place.
Ques. Who went with him?
Ans. Some men, called disciples.
Ques. Why were they called disciples?
Ans. Because they learned of Christ.
Ques. How many disciples did he have?
Ans. Twelve.
Ques. What did Jesus do besides preach?
Ans. He cured the sick.
Ques. Who followed him besides disciples?
Ans. A great many people.
Ques. Why did they follow him?
Ans To hear him preach, and to get him to cure the sick.

Ques. Where did he go one day when he saw a great many people follow him?
Ans. He went up on a mountain.
Ques. What is a mountain?
Ans. A very high hill.
Ques. What did he do there?
Ans. He sat down, and taught his disciples.
Ques. What did he say of the poor in spirit?
Ans. They should have the kingdom of heaven.
Ques. Who are the poor in spirit?
Ans. Those that feel themselves sinners.
Ques. How are such blessed?
Ans. In their spirits.
Ques. What did he say of those that are sorry for their sins?
Ans. They shall be happy.
Ques. Why will those that are sorry for their sins be happy?
Ans. Because Christ will pardon them.
Ques. What did he say of the meek?
Ans. They shall inherit the earth.
Ques. Who are the meek?
Ans. Those that are humble, gentle, and pleasant.
Ques. What very meek man do we read of in the Bible?
Ans. Moses.
Ques. Whom do we call humble?
Ans. Those that are not proud.
Ques. If a boy gets angry at little things, do you think he is meek?
Ans. We do not.
Ques. When you see a little boy or girl proud of nice things, do you think they are meek?
Ans. We do not.
Ques. Which is the happiest, the quiet and pleasant boy, or the fretful one?
Ans. The quiet boy, because everybody loves him.

Ques. Which will be most likely to go to heaven ?
Ans. The quiet and pleasant boy.
Ques. Some good boys and girls wish to be good like Jesus ; what is said of such ?
Ans. They shall be filled with joy and peace.
Ques. What did Jesus say of those that pity, and try to help, the poor ?
Ans. They shall obtain mercy.
Ques. What did he mean by this ?
Ans. That if they become poor and in distress they shall be pitied and helped.
Ques. At whose hand do we all want mercy ?
Ans. At God's hand.

"Oh! how my childhood runs to waste ;
My sins, how great their sum ;
Lord, give me pardon for the past,
And strength for days to come."

LESSON XXXV.

SERMON ON THE MOUNT — CONTINUED.

You have told me, that Jesus Christ taught his disciples that those that are sorry because they are sinners are blessed, and shall go to heaven ; and that the meek shall live long on the earth ; and that those that wish to be good shall be full of joy and peace ; and that the merciful shall obtain mercy.

Ques. Can you tell me what he says of the pure in heart ?
Ans. They shall see God.
Ques. Who are the pure in heart ?
Ans. Those that love God with all the heart.

Ques. Will those whose hearts are pure think about wicked things, and say bad and angry words?

Ans. They will not; for out of the fulness of the heart the mouth speaketh.

Ques. What will you say if your hearts are pure?

Ans.

"I'll leave my sport to read and pray,
And so prepare for heaven"

Ques. Can any but those that have pure hearts see God?

Ans. They cannot, for God commands us to purify our hearts.

Ques. How can we purify our hearts?

Ans. In believing on Christ, and obeying him.

Ques. Should we pray for pure hearts?

Ans. We should pray as David, the pious king, did, "Create in me a clean heart."

Ques. Who are called the children of God?

Ans. Peacemakers.

Ques. If two little children are quarrelling, and a little boy steps forward and tries to stop them and make them happy, what should he be called?

Ans. A peacemaker.

Ques. If a little boy or girl tries to dispute with you, and you should pleasantly speak to him, instead of disputing, what should we call you?

Ans. A peacemaker.

Ques. I have known little boys laugh at good boys that prayed, and tried to be good; were they wicked?

Ans. They were very wicked.

Ques. What does Christ say of those that are laughed at because they pray?

Ans. They shall have the kingdom of heaven.

Ques. What does he tell those to do who are laughed at for praying?

Ans. Rejoice.

Ques. Why should they rejoice?

Ans. Because their names are written in the book of eternal life.

> " Let love through all our actions run,
> And all our words be mild;
> Live like our heavenly Father's son,
> That sweet and lovely child.

> " Now, Lord of all, he reigns above,
> And from his heavenly throne,
> He sees what children dwell in love,
> And marks them for his own."

LESSON XXXVI.

THE LORD'S PRAYER. — CHRIST HEALS THE CENTURION'S SERVANT.

Ques. Good people pray in church, and with their families, both morning and evening; where else should they pray?

Ans. In the closet.

Ques. Who has commanded us to pray in our closet, or in some place by ourselves?

Ans. Jesus Christ.

Ques. To whom should we pray?

Ans. To our Father, which seeth in secret.
Ques. What is promised to those that pray by themselves?
Ans. God shall reward them openly.

Repeat the prayer that Jesus Christ told us to say:— Our Father which art in heaven: hallowed be thy name; Thy kingdom come; Thy will be done on earth as it is in heaven. Give us this day our daily bread; and forgive us our debts, as we forgive our debtors; and lead us not into temptation, but deliver us from evil. For thine is the kingdom, and the power, and the glory, forever. Amen.

Ques. What does the Lord say he will do if we forgive those that wrong us?
Ans. That he will forgive us.
Ques. And if we do not forgive them, what does he say?
Ans. That he will not forgive us.
Ques. After Jesus had taught his disciples this prayer, besides many other things, he came down from the mountain. Can you tell who met him and asked him to cure a sick man?
Ans. The elders of the Jews.
Ques. Who was the sick man that they wanted cured?
Ans. A servant of a rich officer.
Ques. What was this officer called?
Ans. Centurion.
Ques Why were the elders anxious to have Jesus cure this servant?
Ans. Because his master loved the Jews.
Ques. What had he built for them?
Ans. A house of worship.
Ques. How did the officer regard Jesus?
Ans. As a man of great power.
Ques. How did he feel about his coming to his house?
Ans. He felt unworthy to have him come.

Ques. What did he do?
Ans. He sent a servant to say to him, "I am not worthy; only speak, and my servant shall be healed."
Ques. What did Jesus say of this man's faith?
Ans. I have not seen such faith in Israel.
Ques. What is it to have faith?
Ans. To believe.
Ques. What did Jesus do?
Ans. He spake to the servant, and said the sick man was cured.
Ques. What did he command the servant?
Ans. To go back and tell the centurion that it should be just as he believed.
Ques. How was the sick man when the servant got home?
Ans. He was well.
Ques. How was he cured?
Ans. Jesus spake, and he was cured.
Ques. Can a physician cure the sick by speaking?
Ans. He cannot.
Ques. Who can heal the sick, raise the dead in a moment?
Ans.

"The Almighty Maker, God,
  How glorious is his name!
His wonders how diffused abroad,
  Throughout creation's frame!"

LESSON XXXVII.

THE WIDOW'S SON RAISED FROM THE DEAD.

"Come, children, tune your voices
Unto a joyful lay;
Lo! heaven and earth rejoices
On this most happy day."

When Christ healed the rich man's servant that we told you about in the last lesson, he was in Capernaum.

Ques. Where did he go the next day?
Ans. To a town called Nain.
Ques. Who went with him?
Ans. His disciples, and many people.
Ques. What did they see as they opened the gate to go into the town?
Ans. A great many people coming.
Ques. What were some men carrying?
Ans. The dead son of a widow.
Ques. What is a widow?
Ans. A woman whose husband is dead.
Ques. How did the poor widow feel?
Ans. Very bad, for her only son was dead.
Ques. How did Jesus feel for the poor woman when he saw her weeping?
Ans. He pitied her, and said, Weep not.
Ques. What did the men do when Jesus came up to them?
Ans. They stopped.
Ques. What did Jesus do?
Ans. He spoke to the dead man.
Ques. What did he say to him?
Ans. Rise up alive.
Ques. Did the dead man hear him?
Ans. He did, and he rose up and spoke.
Ques. How did the people feel?

Ans. They were afraid.
Ques. What did they call Jesus?
Ans. A prophet.
Ques. What did some say God had fulfilled to them?
Ans. His promise of mercy.
Ques. To whom was this promise made?
Ans. To Adam and Eve.

In the last lesson we learned that Christ healed the servant of a rich man, and in this lesson we hear of his raising to life the son of a poor widow.

Ques. What should this teach us?
Ans. That we should do good both to the rich and the poor.
Ques. How do some people treat the poor?
Ans. With scorn.
Ques. How do these same ones treat the rich?
Ans. Very politely.
Ques. Are such persons Christlike?
Ans. They are not.
Ques. How does God respect both the rich and poor?
Ans. Alike.

" Hosanna be the children's song,
 To Christ, the children's king;
His praise, to whom our souls belong,
 Let all the children sing.

" Hosanna, sound from hill to hill,
 And spread from plain to plain,
While louder, sweeter, clearer still,
 Woods echo to the strain.

" Hosanna, then, our songs shall be;
 Hosanna to our king:
This is the children's jubilee,
 Let all the children sing."

LESSON XXXVIII.

THE WIND AND SEA OBEY CHRIST.

"Gentle Jesus, meek and mild,
Look upon a little child;
Pity my simplicity,
Suffer me to come to thee.

"Fain I would to thee be brought,
Gracious Lord, forbid it not;
Give a little child a place
In the kingdom of thy grace.

"I shall then show forth thy praise
Serve thee all my happy days;
Then the world shall always see
Christ, thy holy child, in me."

Ques. Where did Jesus go one evening with his disciples, in order to get away from the multitude?
Ans. They sailed over a lake.
Ques. What is the name of the lake?
Ans. Gennesareth.
Ques. What is a lake?

Ans. A body of water almost surrounded with land.
Ques. What did Jesus do when he had got into he boat?
Ans. He leaned his head upon a seat and went a sleep.
Ques. Why did he do this?
Ans. Because he was tired.
Ques. What had he been doing all day?
Ans. Preaching, and teaching the people.
Ques. Do you think good men ever get tired when they are teaching us how to be good?
Ans. We do.
Ques. What happened soon after Jesus went to sleep?
Ans. A furious gale of wind blew over the lake.
Ques. What harm does the wind do to boats on the water?
Ans. It frequently sinks them.
Ques. How did the disciples feel when they saw the wind blow so hard that the boat began to sink?
Ans. They were afraid, and called Jesus.
Ques. What did they say to him?
Ans. Lord, save, or we perish.
Ques. What did Jesus do?
Ans. He arose and said to the wind, Be still
Ques. What did he say to the water?
Ans. Cease.
Ques. Did the wind and water obey him?
Ans. They did; the wind stopped blowing and the waves ceased to roll, and all was still.
Ques How did those with Jesus feel?
Ans. They feared and wondered.
Ques. Do the wind and water obey man when speaks to them?
Ans. They do not.
Ques Did the wind and waves hear Christ speak
Ans. They did not; but he restrained them b - power

QUESTION BOOK. 105

"Lord, teach a simple child to pray,
  And then accept my prayer;
For thou canst hear the words I say
  For thou art everywhere.

"Teach me to do the thing that's right,
  And when I sin, forgive;
And make it still my chief delight,
  To serve thee while I live."

LESSON XXXIX.

MORE ABOUT JESUS CHRIST.

Ques. What did Jesus say of little children?
Ans. Suffer little children to come unto me.
Ques. Why should they let them come to him?
Ans For of such is the kingdom of heaven.

Ques. If he wanted little children to come unto him when on earth, does he now in heaven?
Ans. He does.

> "Christ is in heaven, and can I go
> To thank him for his care?"

Teacher.

> "Not yet, but love him here below,
> And thou shalt praise him there."

Ques. What did Jesus do to the little children that were brought to him?
Ans. He took them in his arms and blessed them.
Ques. What did Jesus do for a blind man?
Ans. He opened his eyes so that he could see.
Ques. What did he do for people that could not speak?
Ans. He cured them, so they could speak.

> "Hear him, ye deep; his praise, ye dumb,
> Your loosened tongues employ;
> Ye blind, behold your Saviour come;
> And leap, ye lame, with joy."

Ques. What did he do for a man who had a withered hand?
Ans. He made it whole, like the other.
Ques. What is a withered hand?
Ans. One that is dried up.
Ques. How long did it take Jesus to heal the sick and open the eyes of the blind?
Ans. Only a moment.
Ques. How did he do these things?
Ans. He spake, and it was done.
Ques. Who fed five thousand people in the desert?
Ans. Jesus.
Ques. What did he do before he gave the food to them?
Ans. He looked up to heaven, and blessed it.
Ques. What should this teach us?

Ans. To ask God's blessing on our food.
Ques. Who did the woman of Samaria say had told her all that she had ever done?
Ans. The Saviour.
Ques. Whom did she think he was?
Ans. The Messiah.

" Poor and needy though I be,
God, my Maker, cares for me;
Gives me shelter, clothing, food,
Gives me all I have of good.

" He will listen when I pray,
He is with me night and day;
When I sleep, and when I wake,
Keep me safe for Jesus' sake.

" He who reigns above the sky
Once became as poor as I;
He whose blood for us was shed
Had not where to lay his head."

LESSON XL.

CHRIST TRANSFIGURED.

" His glory shines with beams so bright,
No mortal eye can bear the sight."

Ques. Whom did Jesus take with him when he went upon a mountain to pray?
Ans. Peter, James, and John.
Ques. How did his face look as he prayed?
Ans. It did shine like the sun.
Ques. What was the appearance of his clothes?
Ans. They were white as the light.
Ques. Who came and talked with Jesus?
Ans. Moses and Elias.
Ques. What did they talk about?

Ans. About Jesus being put to death.
Ques. What were Peter and James and John doing while Jesus was praying?
Ans. They were sleeping.
Ques. What did they see when they awoke?
Ans. They saw his glory, and the two men that were with him.
Ques. What did Peter say to Jesus?
Ans. It is good for us to be here.
Ques. Why did he say this?
Ans. Because he was so happy.
Ques. What did he wish to make?
Ans. Three tents to live in.
Ques. Who did he wish to make them for?
Ans. One for Moses, and one for Elias, and one for Jesus.
Ques. Who was Moses?
Ans. The man that led Israel, and with whom God talked when on Mount Sinai.
Ques. Who was Elias?
Ans. The prophet that went to heaven in a chariot of fire.
Ques. How long had Moses and Elias been dead and in heaven?
Ans. Many hundred years.
Ques. What appeared while Peter was talking?
Ans. A bright cloud passed over them.
Ques. What was heard coming from the cloud?
Ans. A voice.
Ques What did it say?
Ans. This is my beloved son, hear him.
Ques. What did Peter and James and John do when they heard this voice?
Ans. They fell on their faces, because they were afraid.
Ques. What did Jesus say when the voice was past?
Ans. Arise, and be not afraid.

Ques. Did they see any one when they looked up?

Ans. They did not.

Ques. Whose voice was it that said, " This is my beloved Son ? "

Ans. The voice of God the Father.

Ques. Was this voice ever heard before, saying, " This is my beloved Son ? "

Ans. It was heard when Jesus was baptized.

Ques. What did Jesus say to his disciples as he came down from the mountain?

Ans. " Tell no man of the vision until I be risen from the dead."

Ques. How did the disciples feel when they learned that Jesus was to be put to death?

Ans. They were sad.

Ques. Who should we try to be like?

Ans.

"I would be like Jesus,
So frequently in prayer;
Alone upon the mountain top,
He met his Father there.

" I want to be like Jesus,
Engaged in doing good;
So that it might be said of me,
That I've done what I could.

" Alas! I'm not like Jesus,
But I will pray to be;
Kind Saviour, take my sinful heart,
And make me more like thee!"

LESSON XLI.

CHRIST'S AGONY IN THE GARDEN OF GETHSEMANE.

"While passing a garden, I paused to hear
A voice faint and plaintive, from one that was near;
The voice of the suff'rer affected my heart,
While pleading in anguish the poor sinner's part

"I listened a moment, then turned me to see
What man of compassion this stranger might be!
I saw him, low kneeling upon the cold ground,
The loveliest being that ever was found.

"So deep were his sorrows, so fervent his prayers,
That down o'er his bosom rolled sweat, blood, and tears
I wept to behold him.— I asked him his name,
He answered, 'T is Jesus! from heaven I came!'

"'I am thy Redeemer! for thee I must die;
The cup is most bitter, but cannot pass by;
Thy sins, like a mountain, are laid upon me;
And all this deep anguish I suffer for thee.'"

Ques. How long did Christ go about preaching and healing the sick, etc.?

Ans. About three years and a half.

Ques. Who hated him, and wished to kill him?

Ans. A great many of the Jews.

Ques. Why did they hate him?

Ans. Because he told them of their sins.

Ques. Did they hate him for any thing else?

Ans. He was humble, and went with the poor.

Ques. Do you think that made them hate him?

Ans. We do, for they were proud, and went with the rich.

Ques. Whose company should we seek?

Ans. The society of the good, whether they are rich or poor.

Ques. What should we do when we are told of our faults?

Ans. We should be sorry, and ask God to make us better.

Ques. Did Jesus know that the Jews wished to kill him?

Ans. He did, for he knows all hearts.

Ques. Where did he go the evening before he was to be crucified?

Ans. Into a grove of olive trees.

Ques. Where was this grove or garden?

Ans. In Gethsemane.

Ques. Why did he go there?

Ans. To pray.

Ques. How did he feel when he kneeled there to pray?

Ans. He was in an agony of spirit.

Ques. Why was his spirit pained?

Ans. Because he felt the sins of the world, and knew he must die for them, or it would be lost.

Ques. What did he ask of his Father?

Ans. Spare me from this hour.

Ques. Did he not wish his Father to do as he pleased?

Ans. He said, "Not my will, but thine, be done."

Ques. What came through the skin and fell to the ground because of his distress?

Ans. Great drops of blood and water.

My little children, you have seen people sweat great drops of sweat when they have been to work hard, but your Saviour sweat great drops of blood for us. Oh, how should we love him!

Ques. Who saw his agony, and came to comfort him?

Ans. An angel.

Ques. Little children, did Christ suffer this for you?

Ans. He did.

Ques. Where were Christ's disciples all this time?

Ans. A little distance from him in the garden.

Ques. Were all of them there?

Ans. Judas was not; he had gone with those that hated Jesus.
Ques. What did he do?
Ans. He told them where they could find Jesus, and went with them, and kissed Jesus, so they might know him from the rest.

LESSON XLII.

THE TRIAL OF JESUS CHRIST.

"Ye that pass by, behold the man!
The man of grief, condemned for you.
The Lamb of God, for sinners slain,
Weeping, to Calvary pursue!

Ques. As Judas led along the murderous band, and came into the garden where Jesus and his disciples were, how did he make them know which was Jesus?
Ans. He kissed him.
Ques. Did Jesus know that Judas did not kiss him because he loved him?
Ans. He did, and he said, Betrayest thou me with a kiss?
Ques. What did the disciples say when they saw so many people come with swords to take Jesus?
Ans. Shall we strike with our swords.
Ques. What did Jesus say?
Ans. No, suffer ye thus far.
Ques. Before Jesus had replied, what had one of the disciples done?
Ans. Struck the servant of the high priest, and cut off his ear.
Ques. What did Jesus then do?
Ans. He healed him.

Ques. If Jesus had had a wicked heart, would he have healed him when he had come to take Jesus and have him killed?

Ans. He would not.

Ques. What should this teach us?

Ans. To bless those that hurt us and wrong us.

Ques. Where did they lead Jesus?

Ans. To the house of the high-priest.

Ques. Which of his disciples followed him there.

Ans. Peter and John.

Ques. Which of them was afraid, and said that he was not Jesus' disciple?

Ans. Peter.

Ques. How many times did he say that he was not a disciple?

Ans. Three times.

Ques. Did Jesus know that Peter denied him?

Ans. He did; he had told him that he would do so.

Ques. What did Peter do after he had denied being a disciple?

Ans. He went out, and wept bitterly.

Ques. What had he done in saying that he was not a disciple?

Ans. He had denied the truth.

Ques. What do we suppose made him deny the truth?

Ans. He was afraid of being hurt or killed.

Ques. What was done to Jesus in the house of the high-priest?

Ans. He was blindfolded and mocked, and some struck him.

Ques. What did they say to him?

Ans. If thou be the Son of God, tell us who smote thee.

Ques. What did the priests say to him?

Ans. Art thou the Son of God.

Ques. What did Jesus answer?

Ans. Ye say that I am.

Ques. What did they then?
Ans. They put irons on his hands, and led him to the governor.
Ques. Who was the governor?
Ans. Pilate.
Ques. What did he do with him?
Ans. He sent him to Herod.

LESSON XLIII.

INCIDENTS PRIOR TO THE CRUCIFIXION.

"Extended on a cursed tree,
Besmeared with dust and sweat and blood,—
See there the King of Glory, see,
Sinks, and expires, the Son of God!"

Ques. What did Herod do with Jesus?
Ans. He mocked him.
Ques. Who was this Herod?
Ans. The son of the wicked Herod that wished to kill Christ when he was an infant.
Ques. Why did they send Christ to him?
Ans. Because he was ruler over Galilee, where Christ lived when at home.
Ques. How did Herod treat Christ?
Ans. He made sport of him.
Ques. What did Herod then do?
Ans. Sent him back to Pilate, the governor of Judea?
Ques. What did Pilate say to the Jews who were clamoring for the blood of Jesus?
Ans. Neither I nor Herod finds guilt in this man.
Ques. What did he wish to do?
Ans. Let him go.
Ques. What did the Jews say?

Ans. They cried, crucify him!
Ques. What is it to crucify?
Ans. To hang upon a cross or tree.
Ques. Did Pilate consent to crucify Jesus?
Ans. He washed his hands, and said, Do as you please, I find no fault in him.
Ques. What did the Jews say?
Ans. We will bear the blame.
Ques. What was done then with Jesus?
Ans. They led him into a large hall, and took off his garments, and put on a scarlet robe.
Ques. What did they put on his head?
Ans. A crown of thorns.

> "See, from his head, his hands, his feet,
> Sorrow and love flow mingled down;
> Did e'er such love and sorrow meet,
> Or thorns compose so rich a crown?"

Ques. What was put in his hand?
Ans. A cane, made of reed.
Ques. Why did they put on a scarlet cloak and crown of thorns?
Ans. To mock him because some said he was king of the Jews.
Ques. Did kings wear scarlet cloaks, and crowns on their heads?
Ans. They did, and carried sceptres in their hands.
Ques. What did they say to him?
Ans. Long live the King of the Jews!
Ques. How did they say this?
Ans. Mockingly.
Ques. What other indignity did they offer to him?
Ans. They spit upon him, and struck him upon his head with a reed.
Ques. Where did they then lead him?
Ans. To the hill Calvary.
Ques. Who followed him there?
Ans. Some people, crying.

" See his temples crowned with thorns,
　His bleeding hands extended wide;
His streaming feet transfixed and torn,
　The fountain gushing from his side.

" Beneath my load he faints and dies,
　I filled his soul with pangs unknown,
I caused those mortal groans and cries
　I killed the Father's only son."

LESSON XLIV.

THE CRUCIFIXION.

"Lo! at noon 't is sudden night,
　Darkness covers all the day;
Rocks are rending at the sight;
　Children, can you tell me why
　　Jesus condescends to die?"

Ques Who followed Jesus up Calvary's hill?
Ans. A great company, weeping for him.

Ques. What did Jesus say to them?
Ans. Weep not for me, but for yourselves and children.
Ques. Why did he tell them to weep for themselves and children?
Ans. Because of the trouble that was to come upon them.
Ques. Who were to be troubled?
Ans. The Jews.
Ques. Why were they to be troubled?
Ans. Because they did not believe in Christ, but put him to death.
Ques. Upon what was Jesus crucified?
Ans. Upon a cross.
Ques. Who was crucified each side of him?
Ans. A thief.
Ques. What is a thief?
Ans. A person that steals.
Ques. What did they give Jesus to drink?
Ans. Vinegar and gall.
Ques. How does gall taste?
Ans. Very bitter.
Ques. Did he drink it?
Ans. He only tasted it.

Dear children, your Saviour was not allowed a drink of cold water, when he was fainting and thirsting; but when he called for drink, they only offered him sour vinegar and bitter gall, which he could not drink, and then they drove nails through his hands and feet to nail him to the cross.

Ques. How did he feel towards those that were nailing him to the cross?
Ans. He forgave them, and prayed for them.
Ques. What should this teach us?
Ans. To forgive, and pray for those that injure us.

Ques. What happened after Jesus had hung upon the cross about three hours?
Ans. Darkness came over all the country.
Ques. How long was it dark?
Ans. Three hours.
Ques. How dark was it?
Ans. So dark that they could not see the sun.
Ques. What time in the day was it dark?
Ans. From twelve o'clock at noon till three o'clock in the afternoon.
Ques. What shook the earth when he bowed his head and died?
Ans. An earthquake.
Ques. What did it do?
Ans. It split the rocks, and opened the graves.
Ques. What happened to the dead in the graves?
Ans. They were made alive and walked.
Ques. What was done to the beautiful Temple?
Ans. Its vail was torn open.
Ques. What was the vail of the temple?
Ans. A beautiful covering over the holy place.
Ques. How did those feel that had put Jesus to death, when they saw the darkness and earthquake, and the dead made alive and walking about?
Ans. They were afraid, and smote their breasts.
Ques. What did they say?
Ans. Truly, this was the Son of God.

> "Was it for crimes that I have done,
> He groaned upon the tree?
> Amazing pity! Grace unknown'
> And love beyond degree.

> "Well might the sun in darkness hide,
> And shut its glories in,
> When Christ the mighty Maker died
> For man the creature's sin!"

LESSON XLV.

CHRIST'S BURIAL AND RESURRECTION.

Ques. As it was drawing near evening, and the next day was the Jewish Sabbath, what did the Jews wish to do?
Ans. To bury Jesus and the two thieves.
Ques. What did the soldiers do to those that were hung, to make them die?
Ans. They broke their legs.
Ques. Did they break Jesus' bones?
Ans. They did not, for he was dead.
Ques. What did a wicked soldier do to Jesus?
Ans. He pierced his side with a spear.
Ques. What run from his pierced side?
Ans. Blood and water.

Children, this was all done for our sake, because of our sins, that we may live in glory.

Ques. How should we feel towards Jesus Christ, who suffered so much for us?
Ans. We should love him with all our hearts.
Ques. Who went to Pilate, and asked for the dead body of Jesus?
Ans. A good man, named Joseph.
Ques. What did he wish to do with it?
Ans. To put it in a nice new tomb.
Ques. Who went to the tomb to see him bury Jesus?
Ans. Some women, and a man named Nicodemus.
Ques. What did they place before the door of the tomb after they had put the body in it?
Ans. A large stone.
Ques. What did the Jews do?
Ans. They sent some soldiers to watch it.
Ques Why did they watch it?

Ans. For fear that the friends of Christ would steal his body, and then say that Christ was risen from the dead.

Ques. How many nights did Christ lay in the tomb?
Ans. Friday and Saturday nights.
Ques. What did the soldiers see on Sunday morning as they were watching the tomb?
Ans. An angel gliding down from the sky.
Ques. What did he do?
Ans. He rolled away the large stone that was before the tomb.
Ques. What did he do then?
Ans. He sat down upon the stone.
Ques. What was seen in the tomb?
Ans. The dead body came to life.
Ques. How were the soldiers affected?
Ans. They fell down with fear.
Ques. Who came to the tomb soon after Jesus had risen from the dead?
Ans. Two women.
Ques. How did they feel when they saw the tomb empty?
Ans. They were afraid the soldiers had carried away the dead body.
Ques. As they looked around, what did they see?
Ans. The angel, with long shining robes.
Ques. What did he say to them?
Ans. Be not afraid, for Jesus is risen from the dead.
Ques. What did the angel tell the women to do?
Ans. To go and tell the disciples that Jesus was alive.
Ques. Did they go?
Ans. They went with joy and fear.
Ques. Who met them as they were going?
Ans. Jesus met them, and said, All hail!
Ques. What did they see in his hands and feet?
Ans. The marks that the nails made when he was nailed to the cross.

> "Never love nor sorrow was
> Like that my Jesus showed;
> See him stretched on yonder cross,
> And crushed beneath our load!"

LESSON XLVI.

THE ASCENSION.

> "Shine to his praise, ye crystal skies.
> The floor of his abode;
> Or veil in shades your thousand eyes,
> Before your brighter God."

Ques. How long did Christ stay upon earth after he rose from the dead?

Ans. Forty days.

Ques. What did he do during this time?

Ans. He told the disciples what they must do.

Ques. What did he say they must do?

Ans. Preach the gospel to every creature, and baptize.

Ques. In whose name were they to be baptized?

Ans. In the name of the Father, and the Son, and the Holy Ghost.

Ques. Who were they to baptize?

Ans. Those that repented of their sins and believed on the Saviour.

Ques. With what did he tell his disciples that they should be baptized?

Ans. With the Holy Ghost.

Ques. Who did he say should go with them?

Ans. He said, "Lo, I am with you."

Ques. How long will he be with those that preach his word?

Ans. Even unto the end of the world.

Ques. After Jesus had told his disciples these things where did he go with them?
Ans. To the Mount of Olives.
Ques. Where is the Mount of Olives?
Ans. South of Jerusalem.
Ques. Near to what place did he go?
Ans. Bethany.
Ques. As he came near to Bethany what did he do?
Ans. He lifted up his hands and blessed them.
Ques. What became of the Saviour after he blessed them?
Ans. He went up into heaven.
Ques. What did the disciples see as they stood gazing up into the skies?
Ans. Two angels.
Ques. What did the angels have on?
Ans. White, shining robes.
Ques. What did they ask the disciples?
Ans. Why stand ye gazing up into heaven.
Ques. What did the angels tell them?
Ans. This same Jesus shall come again.
Ques. When shall Jesus come again?
Ans. At the end of the world.
Ques. What will he do?
Ans. He will take the good to heaven, but he will punish the wicked.
Ques. Shall you and I see him?
Ans. We shall, for every eye shall see him.
Ques. Will he judge us?
Ans. He will, for all we think, do, and say.

"O say, shall I be there,
To see the dreadful glare,
The dreadful sound to hear,
The dreadful heat to bear,
Of falling crags, and rocks, of roaring seas,
Of smoking hills and flaming skies!

"O yes! we all shall be there;
The graves shall open be;

All shall the trumpet hear,
The Judge's face shall see;
In vain shall some upon the mountains call
To hide their heads from him who judges all."

LESSON XLVII.

IS JESUS, AND WHAT IS HE DOING FOR US?

"When I see thee hanging, bleeding,
  Dying on the cruel tree;
Pale in woe, yet interceding
  For the men that murdered thee;
How can I refrain from giving
  Life and soul, and all away,
On thy promise ever living,
  Thee adoring night and day?

"When I see thee upward breaking,
  From the grave, on high to stand,

> And thy rightful empire taking,
>   At the Father's blest right hand,
> Can I longer doubt thy favor,
>   Or thy willingness to bless?
> No, my interceding Saviour,
>   Words can ne'er my hopes express.

Ques. Where is Jesus now?
Ans. Sitting at the right hand of God the **Father.**
Ques. What is he now doing for us?
Ans.

> "Now every suppliant's cry he heeds,
> And for the sinner intercedes."

Ques. Where does he plead for us?
Ans. When we have sinned.
Ques. With whom does he plead?
Ans. God the Father.
Ques. If the Saviour did not plead in our behalf, what would become of us?
Ans. We should die in our sins.

> "Dear Saviour, when I languish,
>   And lay me down to die,
> O, send a shining angel
>   To take me to the sky."

Ques. If we are sorry for our sins, what does he say for us?
Ans. Father, forgive them.
Ques. Does God the Father do as the Saviour asks him?
Ans. He does.

> "The Father, satisfied, forgives;
> The soul, repentant, hears and lives."

Ques. What has Christ sent into the world?
Ans. The Holy Spirit.
Ques. Why has he sent his spirit into the world?
Ans. To reprove the world of righteousness and of judgment to come.

Ques. What is it that makes us feel that we have sinned?
Ans. The Holy Spirit.
Ques. And who pleads with God for our forgiveness?
Ans. Jesus Christ.
Ques. Could we ever be saved if there was no Christ?
Ans. We could not.
Ques. Who gave the Saviour to die for sinners?
Ans. God the Father.
Ques. Did not Jesus give himself?
Ans. He did.

"He laid his glory by;
Forsook his dwelling in the sky,
And by a mean and humble birth,
Became a stranger here on earth."

Ques. How should we feel towards him, who has done so much for us?
Ans. We should love and obey him.
Ques. What does he delight to have us do?
Ans. Ask for clean hearts and right spirits.
Ques. What does he say of those that ask?
Ans. Ye shall receive.

"Ask but his grace, and lo! 't is given;
Ask, and he turns your hell to heaven!
Though sin and sorrow wound my soul,
Jesus thy balm will make it whole."

LESSON XLVIII.

HOW CAN WE GO AND LIVE WITH JESUS?

" Cleanse me from sin, my heart renew,
  O, make me wholly thine ;
Distil thy spirit, Lord, like dew,
  Upon this heart of mine.

" Then shall I early know thy grace,
  Obey thy holy will,
And be prepared to see thy face,
  On yonder Zion's hill."

Ques. Little children, if you wish to go and live **with Jesus** in the bright world above, what kind **of hearts** must you have?

Ans. Clean hearts.

Ques. What will make our hearts clean ?

Ans. The blood of Jesus Christ.

Ques. What must we do, in order to have the **blood of** Christ cleanse our hearts ?

Ans. Ask him for clean hearts.
Ques. How must we ask for clean hearts?
Ans. Believing that he will give them to us.
Ques. If we have clean hearts, how shall we always conduct ourselves?
Ans. With mildness and love.
Ques. Shall we indulge in idleness and mischief if we have clean hearts?
Ans. O no.

> "Idle boys and men are found,
> Standing on the devil's ground."

Ques. If our hearts are clean what shall we hate?
Ans. Sin.
Ques. What is sin?
Ans. Disobedience to God.
Ques. Can we, of ourselves, love God and hate sin?
Ans. O no.

> "So hard our hearts have been,
> They love not Christ, nor grieve for sin."

Ques. Tell me some things you must not do if you mean to go to heaven?
Ans. 1st. We must not deceive. 2d. We must not tell a lie. 3d. We must not quarrel. 4th. We must not get angry. 5th. We must not disobey our parents. 6th. We must not be idle.
Ques. What must you do if you wish to get to heaven?
Ans. 1st. We must speak the truth. 2d. Be kind to every one. 3d. Keep the commandments. 4th. Pray for a clean heart. 5th. Believe we have what we pray for.
Ques. When should we seek for clean hearts?
Ans. When we are young.
Ques. Why should we seek him while young?
Ans. Because God has commanded it.

"'T is easier work, if we begin
To fear the Lord betimes
While sinners, that grow old in sin,
Are hardened in their crimes.

"'T will save us from a thousand snares,
To mind religion young;
Grace will reserve our following years,
And make our virtue strong."

LESSON XLIX.

DESCRIBE THE DESTINY OF THE LOST

"Hear the sinner now lamenting
At the sight of fiercer pain;
Cries and tears he now is venting,
But he weeps and cries in vain,
Greatly mourning
That he ne'er was born again."

Ques. Little children, you have learned what you must do if you would get to heaven. Now tell me what will become of the impenitent?
Ans. They will be shut out of heaven.
Ques. Will they have the company of good people?
Ans. They will not.

"There I see my godly neighbors,
Who were once despised by me;
Now they're clad in dazzling splendor,
Waiting my sad fate to see.
Farewell, neighbors!
Dismal gulf, I'm bound for thee."

Ques. What kind of company will they have?
Ans. The company of liars, thieves, and murderers.
Ques. Where will God turn the wicked?
Ans. Into hell.
Ques. What will he rain upon them?

Ans. Fire and brimstone.
Ques. What will they do in that dreadful place?
Ans. They will weep, and gnash their teeth.
Ques Why will they gnash their teeth?
Ans. Because of their pain.

> "Hail! ye ghosts that dwell in darkness,
> Groaning, rattling of your chains!
> Christ has now pronounced my sentence,
> I'm to dwell in endless pain;
> Down I'm rolling,
> Never to return again."

Ques. How long will the wicked remain in this dreadful place?
Ans. Forever.
Ques. Do we read in the Bible of any that ever went to this place?
Ans. We do; of a rich man named Dives.
Ques. Whom did Dives see when he was in the place of torment?
Ans. Lazarus, in Abraham's bosom.
Ques. Who was Lazarus?
Ans. A poor man that laid at the rich man's gate, and ate his crumbs; and he died and went to heaven, but the rich man died and went to hell.
Ques. Who was Abraham?
Ans. A good man that God loved.
Ques. What is he called?
Ans. The father of the faithful.
Ques. What did the rich man ask of Abraham?
Ans. To send Lazarus to him with a drop of cold water.
Ques. Why did he wish for water?
Ans. To cool his tongue, for he was in flames of fire.
Ques. Did Abraham send Lazarus?
Ans. He could not, because there was a great gulf between them.
Ques. How long will the wicked be tormented?
Ans Night and day, forever.

"There is a dreadful hell,
  And everlasting pains;
There sinners must with devils dwell,
  In darkness, fire, and chains.

"Can such a wretch as I
  Escape this cursed end?
And may I hope, whene'er I die,
  I shall to heaven ascend?

"Then I for grace will pray,
  While I have life and breath;
Lest I should be cut off to-day,
  And sent to eternal death."

LESSON L.

DESCRIBE HEAVEN.

"There is, beyond the sky,
  A heaven of joy and love;
And holy children, when they die,
  Go to that world above."

Ques. What sort of place is heaven?
Ans. A very bright and beautiful place.
Ques. What will make it bright?
Ans. The glory of God.
Ques. What sort of people will be there?
Ans. Holy people.
Ques. What is heaven sometimes called?
Ans. A place of rest.
Ques. Whom shall the people delight to see there?
Ans. God; and his name shall be on their foreheads.
Ques. What will he give to his people?
Ans. An eternal weight of glory.
Ques. Will there be night in heaven?
Ans. There will be no night there, neither candle, neither light of the sun

Ques. What shall light the place?
Ans. The glory of the Lamb.
Ques. Who besides God and holy people are in heaven?
Ans. Shining angels.
Ques. How will the people be clothed?
Ans. In white robes, and crowns on their heads.
Ques. What will they do in heaven?
Ans. Praise God, and sing songs.
Ques. What will they have in their hands?
Ans. Harps of gold.
Ques. What songs will be sung in heaven?
Ans Songs of redeeming love.
Ques. To whom will they sing songs?
Ans. To God and the Lamb.
Ques. Who is meant by the Lamb?
Ans. Jesus Christ.
Ques. Will the people ever be sad in heaven, and weep?
Ans. No; for God shall wipe all tears from their eyes.
Ques. Will people die there?
Ans. No; there will be no more pain nor death there.

> "God's own soft hand shall wipe the tears
> From every weeping eye,
> And pains and groans and griefs and fears,
> And death itself shall die.

Ques. How long shall these happy people live in heaven?
Ans. For ever.

Yes, dear children, those that are so happy as to go to heaven will never again be sad or sorrowful, will never be sick and die, but will always be well and happy. Oh, how much we should praise God for what he has done for us!

Ques. Children, do you think it is an easy matter to get to heaven?

Ans. We do not, for Christ says, Strive to enter in.
Ques. What did he mean by the word strive?
Ans. Try hard.
Ques How must we try?
Ans. Pray, and watch against evil as long as we live

"No chilling winds nor pois'nous breath
 Can reach that healthful shore;
Sickness and sorrow, pain and death,
 Are felt and feared no more.

"There, on those high and flowery plains,
 Our spirits ne'er shall tire;
But in perpetual, joyful strains,
 Redeeming love admire."

LESSON LI.

REVIEW THE LAST SEVENTEEN LESSONS.

Ques. Who is Jesus Christ?
Ans. The Son of God.
Ques. What was his mother's name?
Ans. Mary.
Ques. Where was he born?
Ans. In Bethlehem of Judea.
Ques. Who wished to kill him?
Ans. Herod the King.
Ques. Who named him?
Ans. An angel.
Ques. What was Jesus Christ to be?
Ans. A light to the world.
Ques. How old was Jesus when he began to preach?
Ans. About thirty years old.
Ques. How many disciples did he choose?
Ans. Twelve.

Ques. What did he teach them when he went upon a mountain to preach to the multitude?

Ans. 1st. To be humble. 2d. To be sorry for their sins. 3d. To be mild and pleasant. 4th. To wish to be like God. 5th. To be kind to the poor. 6th. To be pure in heart. 7th. To be at peace with everybody. 8th. To be patient when spoken evil of.

Ques. Who have pure hearts?

Ans. Those that have been cleansed with the blood of Christ, and do as he requires.

Ques. Who shall see God?

Ans. Those that have pure hearts.

Ques. Describe the peacemaker?

Ans. One that will not dispute or quarrel, and tries to persuade others not to do so.

Ques. What is said of the peacemakers?

Ans. They shall be called the children of God.

Ques. What did Jesus do besides preaching?

Ans. He cured the sick, opened the eyes of the blind, unstopped the ears of the deaf, and raised the dead.

Ques. How long did he preach, and do these wonderful things?

Ans. About three years and a half.

Ques. Whose servant did Jesus heal as he came down from the mountain?

Ans. The centurion's servant.

Ques. What is said of him?

Ans. He loved the Jews.

Ques. What had he built for them?

Ans. A house to worship in.

Ques. What did he say when he saw Jesus coming?

Ans. I am not worthy that he should come into my house.

Ques. How did Jesus cure his servant?

Ans. He spake, and he was healed.

Ques. What did Jesus say of the centurion?

Ans. That he was a man of great faith

Ques. Should we not believe all that Jesus has said?
Ans. We should.
Ques. Name some that Jesus raised from the dead?
Ans. The son of a widow, and Lazarus.
Ques. What did Jesus say of little children?
Ans. Suffer little children to come unto me.

> "To him let little children come,
> For he has said they may;
> His bosom then shall be their home,
> Their tears he'll wipe away."

LESSON LII.

REVIEW CONTINUED.

Ques Who disliked Jesus?
Ans. The rulers of the Jews.
Ques. Why did they hate him?
Ans. Because he told them of their faults.
Ques. Should we dislike those who tell us of our faults?
Ans. We should not.
Ques. Did Jesus know that many of the Jews hated him, and wanted to kill him?
Ans. He did; he knew all their thoughts.
Ques. Where did he go to pray one evening?
Ans. Into a garden of olive trees.

> "O garden of Olivet, thou dear, honored spot,
> The fame of thy wonder shall ne'er be forgot;
> The theme most transporting to seraphs above,
> The triumph of sorrow, the triumph of love."

Yes, my dear children, the evening before Christ was crucified, he went away under some olive trees, and there he groaned and wept because of the sin that is in the world, and he knew that unless he died and suffered for us, we should be miserable for ever; and as he prayed, he sweat great drops of blood, which ran down his face and fell to the ground. All this was for us, dear children. Oh, how much we should love him!

Ques. While he was praying, who came to take him?
Ans. The rulers of the Jews.
Ques. Who told them where Jesus could be found?
Ans. Judas, one of Christ's disciples.
Ques. Where did they take him?
Ans. To the house of the high priest.
Ques. What did they do with him there?
Ans. They mocked him, and struck him, and spit upon him.
Ques. What did they say of him?
Ans. He speaketh profanely.
Ques. Where did they take him in the morning?
Ans. To Pilate.
Ques. Why did they take him to Pilate?
Ans. To have him crucify Jesus, because he was governor.
Ques. What is it to crucify?
Ans. To hang.
Ques. What did Pilate say of him?
Ans. I find no fault in him.
Ques. What did Pilate consent to?
Ans. To let the Jews crucify Jesus.
Ques. What did the Jews to mock Jesus?
Ans. They put on him a scarlet robe, and a crown of thorns upon his head.
Ques. What did they put in his hand?
Ans. A reed cane.
Ques. Why did they do this?
Ans. Because this was the manner of dressing kings, and they dressed him so to mock him.
Ques. What did they say to him?
Ans. Hail, King of the Jews.

Ques. What shook the earth when Jesus died?
Ans. An earthquake.
Ques. What was done to the beautiful temple?
Ans. Its covering was torn open.
Ques. What was seen in the grave-yards?
Ans. The graves were opened, and the dead came to life and walked.
Ques. Who buried Jesus?
Ans. A man named Joseph.
Ques. When was he buried?
Ans. Friday evening.
Ques. When did he rise from the dead?
Ans. Sunday morning.
Ques. How long did he stay on the earth after he rose from the dead?
Ans. Forty days.
Ques. Where did he then go?
Ans. To heaven.
Ques. What is he doing there?
Ans. Pleading for us.
Ques. Will he come to earth again?
Ans. He will come to judge the world.
Ques. What will he do with those that disobey him?
Ans. Cast them into hell.
Ques. What will he say to those that have loved and obeyed him?
Ans. Come, ye blessed, enter into joys.

> "Hark, my soul, it is the Lord!
> 'T is thy Saviour; hear his word!
> Jesus speaks; he speaks to thee.
> 'Say, poor sinner, lov'st thou me?
>
> "Thou shalt see my glory soon,
> When the work of faith is done,
> Partner of thy throne shalt be;
> 'Say, poor sinner, lov'st thou me?'"

END.

www.ingramcontent.com/pod-product-compliance
Lightning Source LLC
Chambersburg PA
CBHW030400170426
43202CB00010B/1439